100 Hikes in the
NORTH
CASCADES

**Mt. Baker Area • North Cascades NP • Ross Lake NRA
Pasayten Wilderness • Methow-Chelan**

Ira Spring and Harvey Manning
Maps by Helen Sherman

The Mountaineers
Seattle

THE MOUNTAINEERS: Organized 1906 "... to
explore, study, preserve, and enjoy the
natural beauty of the Northwest."

2 1
7 6 5 4 3 2

Published by The Mountaineers
1011 S.W. Klickitat Way, Suite 107, Seattle, Washington 98134

Published simultaneously in Canada by Douglas & McIntyre, Ltd.,
1615 Venables Street, Vancouver, B.C. V5L 2H1

Manufactured in the United States of America

Edited by Jim Jensen
Layout by Bridget Culligan
Maps by Helen Sherman

Cover photograph: Mt. Baker

Library of Congress Cataloging in Publication Data

Spring, Ira.
    100 hikes in the North Cascades.

    Includes index.
    1. Hiking—Washington (State)—Guide-books.
2. Hiking—Cascade Range—Guide-books.   3. Washington
(State)—Description and travel—   —Guide-books.
4. Cascade Range—Description and travel—Guide-books.
I. Manning, Harvey.   II. Title.   III. Title: One
hundred hikes in the North Cascades.
GV199.42.W2S65   1988   917.97'5   88-9283
ISBN 0-89886-153-5

CONTENTS

Location	*Page*	*Status*

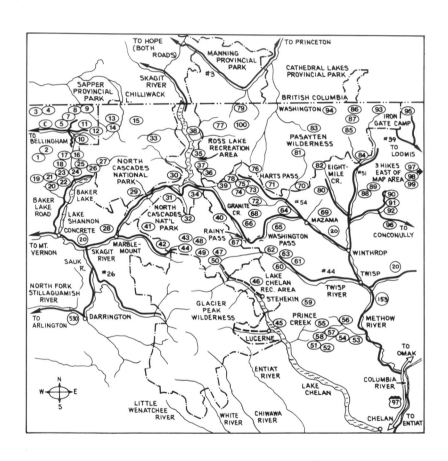

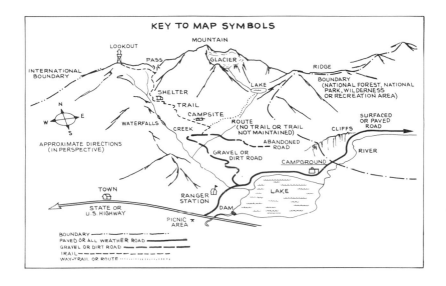

IMPORTANT NOTICE

The Forest Service has renumbered all of the forest roads in Western Washington.

The old numbering system was established more than thirty years ago, before road planners had any notion of the maze of roads that eventually would be developed. The new numbering system should make road directions easier to follow.

To avoid confusion, it is recommended that all Forest Service maps published prior to 1985, with old road numbers, be discarded and new Forest Service maps purchased at any ranger station.

WHERE HAVE OUR TRAILS GONE?

In 1946 the Forest Service inventory showed 144,000 miles of trails in the national forests of America. By 1980 the total had been reduced to 101,000 miles—a loss of 30 percent. The Forest Service would like us to believe this was purely a bookkeeping loss, that the old inventory included stock driveways and wagon roads which weren't real trails anyhow; subtracting these and adding in new-built trails, the reduction was a mere 2 percent.

In other parts of the nation the explanation may or may not be true. Here in the Northwest, there is no covering up the bare-faced fact that the loss of Forest Service trails to logging roads in the state of Washington has been at the very least 30 percent.

Hikers, mainly living in wooden houses and reading and writing books made of paper from wood pulp, freely concede that many of the trails obliterated in the years immediately following World War II were in areas better suited to tree-farming, car-camping, and road-touring than to hiking. (Note that the loss on state and private lands during this period was close to 100 percent.) However, in recent years miles and miles of roads have been built through forests whose timber value was meager but whose value for trail recreation and other roadless-area resources was immense.

The juggernaut rumbles on. The damage of the past decade and a half in the Cascade Range of Washington has been staggering; that planned for the next 15 years would be a catastrophe. In the preferred management alternatives published by the Forest Service, the following miles of trail are jeopardized by new road construction:

Trails in Jeopardy

Okanogan National Forest: 381 miles or 62% of their non-wilderness trails

Wenatchee National Forest: 966 miles or 78% of their non-wilderness trails

Mt. Baker-Snoqualmie National Forest: 484 miles or 48% of their non-wilderness trails

Gifford Pinchot National Forest: 544 miles or 78% of their non-wilderness trails

Total: 2375 miles in jeopardy

Forest Service explainers claim those figures lie, that many of the miles will be on temporary logging roads which afterward will revert to trails, that on some steep hillsides no road at all will be built, the logging done by helicopters. Perhaps—*if* hikers and environmental groups watch the logging plans like hawks.

The explainers further declare that many miles of the "jeopardy" trails are perfectly safe except for a very few feet of their length where they are crossed by roads. Using this defense, Okanogan and Wenatchee National Forests promise that not more than two percent of their trails will be lost to roads. This figure: though a hiker can be happy enough on a trail that starts out in or through a clearcut, a road crossing makes it useless to him; road-broken trails are not maintained for hikers, but for motorcyclists.

OBITUARY

The following is a partial list of trails that have been either obliterated or drastically shortened by logging roads.

MT. BAKER-SNOQUALMIE NATIONAL FOREST

Anderson Butte	8 miles	Barclay Creek	5 miles
Mallardy Ridge	10 miles	Lennox Creek	7 miles
Boardman Lake	5 miles	Sunday Lake	4 miles
Finney Peak	7 miles	Lake Calligan	5 miles
Johnson Ridge	3½ miles	Twin Lakes	2½ miles
Rapid River	5½ miles	Taylor River	10 miles
Deckler River	13 miles	Kelcema Lake	4 miles
Tonga Ridge	5 miles	North Fork Skykomish	7 miles
Foss River	8 miles	Canyon Creek	15 miles
Miller River	5½ miles	Three Fingers	8 miles

WENATCHEE NATIONAL FOREST

Keechelus Ridge	9 miles	Beverly Creek	3 miles
Box Canyon	6 miles	Standup Creek	4 miles
Knox Creek trails	10 miles	Red Top Mountain	14 miles
Amabilis Mountain	6 miles	Chumstick	12 miles
Van Epps Pass	4 miles	Sugar Loaf	3 miles
Jolley Creek	4½ miles	Smith Brook	3½ miles
Cle Elum Ridge	12 miles	Mill Creek	6 miles
Hex Mountain	10½ miles	Tye River	12.3 miles

OKANOGAN NATIONAL FOREST

Gold Creek trails	15 miles	Early Winters	15 miles
Libby Lake	6 miles	Lookout Mountain	6 miles
Granite Creek	20 miles		

GIFFORD PINCHOT NATIONAL FOREST

Burnt Butte	10 miles	Smith Creek Butte	11½ miles
Juniper Ridge	6 miles	Willame	9 miles
Dark Meadow	18 miles	Davis Mountain	4 miles
East Canyon Creek	10 miles	Silver Creek	19 miles
Lewis River	25 miles	Skate Creek	14 miles
Ridge Trail	14 miles	5030 Trail	6 miles
Canyon Creek	13 miles	North Fork Cispus	12 miles
St. Helens Way	8 miles	Bean Creek	10 miles
Muddy River	12 miles	Spirit Lake-Guler	48 miles

SAVING OUR TRAILS
Preservation Goals for the 1990s and Beyond

In the early 1960s The Mountaineers began publishing trail guides as another means of working "to preserve the natural beauty of Northwest America," through putting more feet on certain trails, in certain wildlands. We suffered no delusion that large numbers of boots improve trails or enhance wildness. However, we had learned to our rue that "you use it or lose it," that threatened areas could only be saved if they were more widely known and treasured. We were criticized in certain quarters for contributing to the deterioration of wilderness by publicizing it, and confessed the fault, but could only respond, "Which would you prefer? A hundred boots in a virgin forest? Or that many snarling wheels in a clearcut?"

As the numbers of wilderness lovers have grown so large as to endanger the qualities they love, the rules of "walking light" and "camping no trace" must be the more faithfully observed. Yet the ultimate menace to natural beauty is not hikers, no matter how destructive their boots may be, nor even how polluting their millions of *Giardia* cysts, but doomsday, arriving on two or three or four or six or eight wheels, or on tractor treads, or on whirling wings—the total conquest of the land and water and sky by machinery.

Victories Past

Conceived in campfire conversations of the 1880s, Olympic National Park was established in 1938, the grandest accomplishment of our most conservation-minded president, Franklin D. Roosevelt. (Confined to a wheelchair and never himself able to know the trails with his own feet, FDR nevertheless saw the fallacy in the sneering definition of wilderness areas as "preserves for the aristocracy of the physically fit," knew the value of dreams that never could be personally attained.)

A renewal of the campaigns after World War II brought—regionally, in 1960—the Glacier Peak Wilderness and—nationally, in 1964—the Wilderness Act whereby existing and future wildernesses were placed beyond the fickleness of bureaucracies, guarded by Congress and the President against thoughtless tampering.

1968 was the year of the North Cascades Act, achieving another vision of the nineteenth century, the North Cascades National Park, plus the Lake Chelan and Ross Lake National Recreation Areas, Pasayten Wilderness, and additions to the Glacier Peak Wilderness.

In 1976 the legions of citizens laboring at the grass roots, aided by the matching dedication of certain of their congressmen and senators, obtained the Alpine Lakes Wilderness.

And in 1984 the same alliance, working at the top and at the bottom and all through the middle, all across the state, won the Washington Wilderness Act encompassing more than 1,000,000 acres, including, in the purview of this volume, three new wildernesses—Lake Chelan-Sawtooth, Mt. Baker, and Noisy-Diobsud; additions to the Pasayten

Trail sign on Cathedral Driveway (Hike 96)

Wilderness; and a Mt. Baker National Recreation Area and a North Cascades Scenic Highway Corridor.

Is, therefore, the job done?

Goals Ahead

Absolutely not.

Had hikers been content with the victory of 1938 there never would have been those of 1960, 1968, 1976, and 1984. The American nation as a whole has a step or two yet to go before attaining that condition of flawless perfection where it fits seamlessly into the final mosaic of the Infinite Plan, and the same is true of the National Wilderness Preservation System. In the trail descriptions of this book we have expressed some of the more prominent discontents with the 1984 Act.

Among the omissions are the Alma-Copper and Hidden Lake areas,

11

adjacent to the North Cascades National Park; Beaver Meadows, Tiffany Mountain, and Chopaka Mountain, near the Okanogan; and the Golden Horn area near the North Cascades Highway.

There also are faults of omission from the newly created wildernesses: from the Noisy-Diobsud Wilderness, the lower reaches of its two namesake creeks, the Upper Baker River, and Rocky and Thunder Creeks; from the Mt. Baker Wilderness, Damfino Creek, Church Mountain, Warm Creek, and Shuksan Lake; from the Lake Chelan-Sawtooth Wilderness, Foggy Dew, Safety Harbor, and Eagle Creeks on the south, and Cedar Creek on the north.

The existing Pasayten Wilderness still does not enclose the upper Methow River, lower Lost River, South Twentymile Peak, and the Chewack River at Thirtymile Campground.

The North Cascades Scenic Highway gives only modest protection; at that, it leaves out upper Canyon Creek, upper East Creek, and Driveway Butte.

As for the Mt. Baker National Recreation Area, it was specifically designed to permit snowmobiles to go to the very summit.

—And the above is only a very partial list of the remaining tasks. A very notable—and notorious—remaining problem is the management of the Lake Chelan National Recreation Area, and its failure, to date, to give the Stehekin Valley the care expected of the 1968 North Cascades Act.

It needs to be kept uppermost in mind that designation as "wilderness" or "national park" or "national recreation area" is a means, not the end. The goals ahead are not words on a document or lines on a map but the protection of the land these symbols may signify. Any other symbols that do the job are satisfactory. The *protection* is the thing.

In contrast to the immediate past, the preservationist agenda of the immediate future (that is, the coming several years) is focused less on redrawing maps than employing any practical method to preserve roadless areas from further invasion by machinery. In fact, we are now at a stage where the saving of trails, important though that is, has a lower priority than the saving of fisheries and wildlife resources, scientific values, gene pools, and another contribution of wildland too long neglected, the provision of dependable and pure water for domestic and agricultural needs.

What in the World Happened to Us?

The wheel is more than the symbol. It is the fact. The National Wilderness Act so recognizes by banning "mechanized travel," including *but not limited to* motorized travel; bicycles—"mountain bikes"—are excluded too, for the simple reason that in appropriate terrain they readily can go 5–10 miles per hour, an "unnatural" speed often incompatible with the "natural" 1–3 miles per hour of the traveler on foot.

Outside the boundaries of dedicated wilderness, many trails can be amicably shared by bicycles and pedestrians, both capable of being quiet and minimally destructive and disruptive of the backcountry scene. Attach a motor to the wheels, however, and the route no longer deserves to be called a "trail," it becomes a *road*.

In the past quarter-century conservationists have been busy saving Washington trails by creating a new national park and a bouquet of new wildernesses. Meanwhile, the U.S. Forest Service, without benefit of environmental impact statements, has been assiduously converting *true trails* (that is, paths suitable for speeds of perhaps up to 5 or so miles per hour, the pace of a horse) to *motorcycle roads* (that is, "trails" built to let off-road vehicles—the ORV—do 15–30 miles per hour).

In this quarter-century the concerted efforts of tens of thousands of conservationists protected large expanses of wildland from invasion by machines—but during the same period a comparative handful of ORVers have taken away more miles of trails, converted them to de facto roads, than the conservationists have saved. As the score stands in 1987, only 45 percent of Washington trails are machine-free by being in national parks and wildernesses; of the other 55 percent, half are open to motorcycles—and thus are not truly trails at all.

When automobiles arrived in America the citizenry and government were quick to see they should not be permitted on sidewalks. The Forest Service (and let it be added, the Washington State Department of Natural Resources, or DNR) are slower to recognize that whenever there are more than a few scattered travelers of either kind the difference in speed and purpose between motorized wheels and muscle-powered feet is irreconcilable.

Thinking to serve the laudable purpose of supplying "a wide spectrum of recreational opportunities," the Forest Service initially tolerated ORVs, then began encouraging them, widening and straightening and smoothing "multiple-use trails" to permit higher speeds, thus increasing the number of motors and discouraging hikers, in the end creating "single-purpose ORV trails"—in a word, roads.

Federal funds were employed for the conversion until that source dried up; since 1979 the Forest Service has relied heavily on money from the State of Washington Interagency for Outdoor Recreation (IAC), the subject of the following section of this book.

Certainly, the Forest Service could not engage in such large-scale, long-term conversion of trails to roads if hikers were given the respect their numbers—overwhelming compared to the motorcyclists—deserve.

Hikers spoke up for the Washington Wilderness Act of 1984. By the many thousands they wrote letters to congressmen and senators. The pen is mightier than the wheel, and it must be taken up again, by those same tens of thousands, to write letters to congressmen and senators, with copies to the Regional Forester, Region 6, U.S.F.S., 319 S.W. Pine Street, P.O. Box 3623, Portland, Oregon 97208, asking that:

1. Trails be considered a valuable resource, treated as a separate category in all Forest Plans.
2. All trail users should be notified of public meetings concerning any Forest plan affecting trails; public meetings should be held in metropolitan areas as well as in small, remote communities near the trails.
3. To eliminate the conflict between hikers and ORVs, the concept of multiple-use must be dropped and separate ORV trails built out of sound and sight of hikers and horse-riders.

INTRODUCTION

Broad, smooth, well-marked, heavily traveled, ranger-patroled paths safe and simple for little kids and elderly folks with no mountain training or equipment, or even for monomaniacs dashing from Canada to Mexico. Mean and cruel and mysterious routes through evil brush, over fierce rivers, up shifty screes and moraines to treacherous glaciers and appalling cliffs where none but the skilled and doughty should dare, or perhaps the deranged. Flower strolls for an afternoon, heroic adventures for a week.

A storm side (the west) where precipitation is heavy, winter long, snows deep, glaciers large, peaks sharply sculptured, vegetation lush, and high-country hiking doesn't get comfortably underway until late July. A lee side, a rainshadow side (the east) where clouds are mostly empties, summer is long, vegetation sparse, ridges round and gentle, and meadows melt free of the white by late June.

Places as thronged as a city park on Labor Day, places as lonesome as the South Pole that Scott knew. Scenes that remind of the High Sierra, scenes that remind of Alaska.

In summary, to generalize about the North Cascades: To generalize about the North Cascades is foolish.

Rules, Regulations, and Permits

Except for blocks of state (Department of Natural Resources) land around Chopaka Mountain, scattered enclaves of private lands mostly dating from mining and homestead days, and such miscellaneous bits as the Seattle City Light holdings on the Skagit River, the entirety of the northernmost section of the North Cascades is federally administered. The U.S. Forest Service is the principal trustee, responsibility shared by Mt. Baker-Snoqualmie, Wenatchee, and Okanogan National Forests. Since 1968 the National Park Service has been on the scene in the North Cascades National Park and the accompanying Ross Lake and Lake Chelan National Recreation Areas, essentially parts of the park but permitting some activities, such as hunting, banned within the park proper.

Most of the national forest lands are under "multiple-use" administration, with roads, with logging, mining, and other economic exploitation, and with motorcycles allowed on (too) many trails. Some areas, however, have statutory protection within the National Wilderness Preservation System, where the Wilderness Act of 1964 guarantees that "the earth and its community of life are untrammeled by man, where man himself is a visitor who does not remain." The Glacier Peak Wilderness was established in 1960 and the Pasayten Wilderness in 1968. The Washington Wilderness Act of 1984 made additions to these two wildernesses and in the far north of the North Cascades established these new ones: Mt. Baker, Noisy-Diobsud, and Lake Chelan-Sawtooth. Within these, motorized travel is banned, as is any mechanized travel, such as "mountain bikes." Horse travel is carefully regulated, and though wilderness permits have been discontinued for hikers, they are subject to restrictions on party size and camping, and must acquaint themselves with the travel regulations before setting out.

The North Cascades National Park, established in 1968, was set aside, to use the words of the National Park Act of 1916, "to conserve the scenery and the natural and historic objects and the wildlife . . . " Each visitor therefore must enjoy the park "in such manner and by such means as will leave it unimpaired for the enjoyment of future generations." Most of the park is intended to be further covered by the Wilderness Act, giving a still higher degree of protection.

To help attain these goals, the Park Service requires each trail user to have a backcountry permit that must be shown on request to a backcountry ranger. Permits may be obtained by mail from the Park Service or in person from ranger stations on the major entry roads.

Maps

Each hike description in this book lists the appropriate topographic maps published by the U.S. Geological Survey. These can be purchased at map stores or mountaineering equipment shops or by writing the U.S. Geological Survey, Federal Center, Denver, Colorado 80225.

The national forests and the park publish recreation maps that are quite accurate, up-to-date, and inexpensive. Forest Service maps may be obtained at ranger stations or by writing:

Mt. Baker-Snoqualmie National Forest
1022 1st Avenue
Seattle, WA 98104

Wenatchee National Forest
P.O. Box 811
Wenatchee, WA 98801

Okanogan National Forest
P.O. Box 950
Okanogan, WA 98840

Park Service maps may be obtained, along with backcountry permits, at the ranger stations at Sedro Woolley, Marblemount, Chelan, and Stehekin.

In the national forests a traveler not only must have a map published by the Forest Service but must have a *current* map. The problem is that the Forest Service has renumbered roads, made necessary when the number of roads grew so large as to require the use of more than three digits. For instance, a spur road from Road No. 12 becomes road No. 1200830, and is perhaps shown as such on the new map, though the roadside sign may be simply "830." One ranger district is using parentheses, as (1200)830, another dashes, as 1200-830, and another commas, as 1200,830.

A traveler *must* know the right numbers because in many areas the Forest Service puts no names on signs, just numbers—the new ones. Your map, if it had the old numbers, will merely deepen your confusion. Any map older than 1985 should be replaced.

Clothing and Equipment

Many trails described in this book can be walked easily and safely, at least along the lower portions, by any person capable of getting out of a car and onto his feet, and without any special equipment whatever. To such people we can only say, "welcome to walking—but beware!" Northwest mountain weather, especially on the ocean side of the ranges, is notoriously undependable. Cloudless morning skies can be followed by afternoon deluges of rain or fierce squalls of snow. Even without a storm a person can get mighty chilly on high ridges when—as often happens—a cold wind blows under a bright sun and pure blue sky.

No one should set out on a Cascade trail, unless for a brief stroll, lacking warm long pants, wool (or the equivalent) shirt or sweater, and a windproof and rain-repellent parka, coat, or poncho. (All these in the rucksack, if not on the body during the hot hours.) And on the feet—sturdy shoes or boots plus wool socks and an extra pair of socks in the rucksack.

As for that rucksack, it should also contain the Ten Essentials, found to be so by generations of members of The Mountaineers, often from sad experience:

1. Extra clothing—more than needed in good weather.
2. Extra food—enough so something is left over at the end of the trip.
3. Sunglasses—necessary for most alpine travel and indispensable on snow.
4. Knife—for first aid and emergency firebuilding (making kindling).
5. Firestarter—a candle or chemical fuel for starting a fire with wet wood.
6. First aid kit.
7. Matches—in a waterproof container.
8. Flashlight—with extra bulb and batteries.
9. Map—be sure it's the right one for the trip.
10. Compass—be sure to know the declination, east or west.

Camping and Fires

Indiscriminate camping blights alpine meadows. A single small party may trample grass, flowers, and heather so badly they don't recover from the shock for several years. If the same spot is used several or more times a summer, year after year, the greenery vanishes, replaced by bare dirt. The respectful traveler always aims to camp in the woods, or in rocky morainal areas. These alternatives lacking, it is better to use a meadow site already bare—in technical terminology, "hardened"—rather than extend the destruction into virginal places nearby.

Particularly to be avoided are camps on soft meadows on the banks of streams and lakes (hard rock or bare-dirt or gravel sites may be quite all right). Delightful and scenic as waterside meadows are, their use may endanger the water purity, as well as the health of delicate plants. Further, no matter how "hard" the site may be, a camp on a viewpoint makes the beauty unavailable to other hikers who simply want to come and look, or eat lunch, and then go camp in the woods.

Carry a collapsible water container to minimize the trips to the water

Early fall snowstorm near summit of Dollar Watch Mountain (Hike 83)

supply that beat down a path. (As a bonus, the container lets you camp high on a dry ridge, where the solitude and the views are.)

Carry a lightweight pair of camp shoes, less destructive to plants and soils than trail boots.

As the age of laissez faire camping yields to the era of thoughtful management, different policies are being adopted in different places. For example, high-use spots may be designated "Day Use Only," forbidding camps. In others there is a blanket rule against camps within 100 to 200 feet of the water. However, in certain areas the rangers have inventoried existing camps, found 95 percent are within 100 feet of the water, and decided it is better to keep existing sites, where the vegetation long since has been gone, than to establish new "barrens" elsewhere. The rule in such places is "use established sites"; wilderness rangers on their rounds dis-establish those sites judged unacceptable.

Few shelter cabins remain—most shown on maps aren't there anymore—so always carry a tent or tarp. *Never* ditch the sleeping area unless and until essential to avoid being flooded out—and afterward be sure to fill the ditches, carefully replacing any sod that may have been dug up.

Always carry a sleeping pad of some sort to keep your bag dry and your bones comfortable. *Do not* revert to the ancient bough bed of the frontier past.

The wood fire also is nearly obsolete in the high country. At best, dry firewood is hard to find at popular camps. What's left, the picturesque silver snags and logs, is part of the scenery, too valuable to be wasted cooking a pot of soup. It should be (but isn't quite, what with the survival of little hatchets and little folks who love to wield them) needless to say that green, living wood must never be cut; it doesn't burn anyway.

Both for reasons of convenience and conservation, the highland hiker should carry a lightweight stove for cooking (or he should not cook—

though the food is cold, the inner man is hot) and depend on clothing and shelter (and sunset strolls) for evening warmth. The pleasures of a roaring blaze on a cold mountain night are indisputable, but a single party on a single night may use up ingredients of the scenery that were long decades in growing, dying, and silvering.

At remote backcountry camps, and in forests, fires perhaps may still be built with a clear conscience. Again, one should minimize impact by using only established fire pits and using only dead and down wood. When finished, be certain the fire is absolutely out—drown the coals and stir them with a stick and then drown the ashes until the smoking and steaming have stopped completely and a finger stuck in the slurry feels no heat. Embers can smoulder underground in dry duff for days, spreading gradually and burning out a wide pit—or kindling trees and starting a forest fire.

If you decide to build a fire, *do not make a new fire ring*—use an existing one. In popular areas patroled by rangers, its existence means this is an approved, "established" or "designated" campsite. If a fire ring has been heaped over with rocks, it means the site has been dis-established.

Litter and Garbage and Sanitation

Ours is a wasteful, throwaway civilization—and something is going to have to be done about that soon. Meanwhile, it is bad wildland manners to leave litter for others to worry about. The rule among considerate hikers is: *If you can carry it in full, you can carry it out empty.*

Thanks to a steady improvement in manners over recent decades, and the posting of wilderness rangers who glory in the name of garbage-collectors, American trails are cleaner than they have been since Columbus landed. Every hiker should learn to be a happy collector.

On a day hike, take back to the road (and garbage can) every last orange peel and gum wrapper.

On an overnight or longer hike, burn all paper (if a fire is built) but carry back all unburnables, including cans, metal foil, plastic, glass, and papers that won't burn.

Don't bury garbage. If fresh, animals will dig it up and scatter the remnants. Burning before burying is no answer either. Tin cans take as long as 40 years to disintegrate completely; aluminum and glass last for centuries. Further, digging pits to bury junk disturbs the ground cover, and iron eventually leaches from buried cans and "rusts" springs and creeks.

Don't leave leftover food for the next travelers; they will have their own supplies and won't be tempted by "gifts" spoiled by time or chewed by animals.

Especially don't cache plastic tarps. Weathering quickly ruins the fabric, little creatures nibble, and the result is a useless, miserable mess.

Keep the water pure. Don't wash dishes in streams or lakes, loosing food particles and detergent. Haul buckets of water off to the woods or rocks, and wash and rinse there. Eliminate body wastes in places well removed from watercourses; first dig a shallow hole in the "biological disposer layer," then, if the surroundings are certainly non-flammable, touch a match to the toilet paper (or better, use leaves), and finally cover the evidence. So managed, the wastes are consumed in a matter of days. Where privies are provided, use them.

Water

Hikers traditionally have drunk the water in wilderness in confidence, doing their utmost to avoid contaminating it so the next person also can safely drink. But there is no assurance your predecessor has been so careful.

No open water ever, nowadays, can be considered certainly safe for human consumption. Any reference in this book to "drinking water" is not a guarantee. It is entirely up to the individual to judge the situation and decide whether to take a chance.

In the late 1970s a great epidemic of giardiasis began, caused by a vicious little parasite that spends part of its life cycle swimming free in water, part in the intestinal tract of beavers and other wildlife, dogs, and people. Actually, the "epidemic" was solely in the press; *Giardia* were first identified in the 18th century and are present in the public water systems of many cities of the world and many towns in America—including some in the foothills of the Cascades. Long before the "outbreak" of "beaver fever" there was the well-known malady, the "Boy Scout trots." This is not to make light of the disease; though most humans feel no ill effects (but become carriers), others have serious symptoms which include devastating diarrhea, and the treatment is nearly as unpleasant. The reason giardiasis has become "epidemic" is that there are more people in the backcountry—more people drinking water contaminated by animals—more people contaminating the water.

Whenever in doubt, boil the water 10 minutes. Keep in mind that *Giardia* can survive in water at or near freezing for weeks or months—a snow pond is not necessarily safe. Boiling is 100 percent effective against not only *Giardia* but the myriad other filthy little blighters that may upset your digestion or—as with some forms of hepatitis—destroy your liver.

If you cannot boil, use one of the several *iodine* treatments (chlorine compounds have been found untrustworthy in wildland circumstances), such as Potable Aqua or the more complicated method that employs iodine crystals. Rumor to the contrary, iodine treatments pose no threat to the health.

Be very wary of the filters sold in backpacking shops. The technology is steadily advancing and several products already offer some protection, but most filters as of 1987 are a snare and a delusion.

Party Size

One management technique used to minimize impact in popular areas is to limit the number of people in any one group to a dozen or fewer. Hikers with very large families (or outing groups from clubs or wherever) should check the rules when planning a trip.

Pets

The handwriting is on the wall for dog owners. Pets always have been forbidden on national park trails and now some parts of wildernesses are being closed. How fast the ban spreads will depend on the owners' sensitivity, training, acceptance of responsibility, and courtesy—and on the expressed wishes of non-owners.

Where pets are permitted, even a well-behaved dog can ruin someone else's trip. Some dogs noisily defend an ill-defined territory for their master, "guard" him on the trail, snitch enemy bacon, and are quite likely to defecate on the flat bit of ground the next hiker will want to sleep on.

For a long time to come there will be plenty of "empty" country for those who hunt upland game with dogs or who simply can't enjoy a family outing without ol' Rover. However, the family that wants to go where the crowds are must leave its best friend home.

Do not depend on friendly tolerance of wilderness neighbors. Some people are so harassed at home by loose dogs that a hound in the wilderness has the same effect on them as a motorcycle. They may holler at you and turn you in to the ranger.

Dogs belong to the same family as coyotes, and even if no wildlife is visible, a dog's presence is sensed by the small wild things into whose home it is intruding.

Horses

As the backcountry population has grown, encounters between hikers and horse-riders have increased. Even though hikers are unhappy when a trail has been damaged by horses or find campsites that look like barnyards, most hikers enjoy seeing the animals and accept them as part of the wilderness experience.

Most horse riders do their best to be good neighbors on the trail and know how to go about it. The typical hiker, though, is ignorant of the difficulties inherent in maneuvering a huge mass of flesh (containing a very small brain) along narrow paths on steep mountains.

The first rule is, the horse has the right of way. For his own safety as well as that of the rider, the hiker must get off the trail—on the downhill side, preferably, giving the heavy animal and its rider the inside of the tread. If necessary—as, say, on a steep hillside—retreat some distance to a safe passing point.

The second rule is, when you see the horse approaching, do not keep silent or stand still in a mistaken attempt to avoid frightening the beast. Continue normal motions and speak to it, so the creature will recognize you as just another human and not think you a silent and doubtless dangerous monster.

Finally, if you have a dog along, get a tight grip on its throat to stop the nipping and yapping, which may endanger the rider and, in the case of a surly horse, the dog as well.

Theft

A quarter-century ago theft from a car left at the trailhead was rare. Not now. Equipment has become so fancy and expensive, so much worth stealing, and hikers so numerous, their throngs creating large assemblages of valuables, that theft is a growing problem. Not even wilderness camps are entirely safe; a single raider hitting an unguarded camp may easily carry off several sleeping bags, a couple tents and assorted stoves, down booties, and freeze-dried strawberries—maybe $1000 worth of gear in one load! However, the professionals who do most of the stealing mainly concentrate on cars. Authorities are concerned but can't post guards at every trailhead.

Rangers have the following recommendations.

First and foremost, don't make crime profitable for the pros. If they break into a hundred cars and get nothing but moldy boots and tattered T shirts they'll give up. The best bet is to arrive in a beat-up 1960 car with doors and windows that don't close and leave in it nothing of value. If you insist on driving a nice new car, at least don't have mag wheels, tape deck, and radio, and keep it empty of gear. Don't think locks help—pros can open your car door and trunk as fast with a picklock as you can with your key. Don't imagine you can hide anything from them—they know all the hiding spots. If the hike is part of an extended car trip, arrange to store your extra equipment at a nearby motel.

Be suspicious of anyone waiting at a trailhead. One of the tricks of the trade is to sit there with a pack as if waiting for a ride, watching new arrivals unpack—and hide their valuables—and maybe even striking up a conversation to determine how long the marks will be away.

The ultimate solution, of course, is for hikers to become as poor as they were in the olden days. No criminal would consider trailheads profitable if the loot consisted solely of shabby khaki war surplus.

Safety Considerations

The reason the Ten Essentials are advised is that hiking in the backcountry entails unavoidable risk that every hiker assumes and must be aware of and respect. The fact that a trail is described in this book is not a representation that it will be safe for you. Trails vary greatly in difficulty and in the degree of conditioning and agility one needs to enjoy them safely. On some hikes routes may have changed or conditions may have deteriorated since the descriptions were written. Also, trail conditions can change even from day to day, owing to weather and other factors. A trail that is safe on a dry day or for a highly conditioned, agile, properly equipped hiker may be completely unsafe for someone else or unsafe under adverse weather conditions.

You can minimize your risks on the trail by being knowledgeable, prepared and alert. There is not space in this book for a general treatise on safety in the mountains, but there are a number of good books and public courses on the subject and you should take advantage of them to increase your knowledge. Just as important, you should always be aware of your own limitations and of conditions existing when and where you are hiking. If conditions are dangerous, or if you are not prepared to deal with them safely, choose a different hike! It's better to have a wasted drive than to be the subject of a mountain rescue.

These warnings are not intended to scare you off the trails. Hundreds of thousands of people have safe and enjoyable hikes every year. However, one element of the beauty, freedom, and excitement of the wilderness is the presence of risks that do not confront us at home. When you hike you assume those risks. They can be met safely, but only if you exercise your own independent judgement and common sense.

Volunteers for Outdoor Washington

For 10,000 years or so the only trails in the North Cascades were those beaten out by the feet of deer, elk, bear, coyotes, marmots, and the folks

Mount Baker from Iceberg Lake (Hike 17)

who had trekked on over from Asia. For some 50 years, starting in the late 19th century, the "dirty miners in search of shining gold" built and maintained hundreds of miles of trails, often wide and solid enough for packtrains. During the same period many a valley had a trapline, a trapper, and a trapper's trail, and many a ridge had a sheepherder's driveway. For 30-odd years, roughly from World War I to World War II, U.S. Forest Service rangers built trails to serve fire lookouts atop peaks and to give firefighting crews quick walking to blazes. In the late 1930s the trail system attained its maximum mileage and excellence.

Then the rangers began taking to airplanes and parachutes and the miners to helicopters and the trail system began to deteriorate. Eventually the Forest Service expanded the concept of multiple-use to encompass spending money on trails where recreation was the main or only use, instead of a subsidiary one as was formerly the case. Just about that time the United States fell on hard times and the funds for Forest Service—and Park Service—trails were largely diverted to maintaining troops in foreign nations.

Volunteers for Outdoor Washington (VOW) is part of the national trend toward construction and maintenance of trails by unpaid volunteers. The principle is simple: If each hiker spends several days a year working on a crew, trails can continue to be easily walked that otherwise would be abandoned by the government for lack of money. So, would you rather devote some days to whacking at slide alder with an ax or cutting through windfall with a saw, or would you rather devote tortured hours to hauling your pack through brush and crawling over logs?

For information on how your organization, or you as an individual, can join the VOW effort, contact Volunteers for Outdoor Washington, 607 3rd Avenue, Room 210, Seattle, Washington 98104.

Protect This Land, Your Land

The Cascade country is large and rugged and wild—but it is also, and particularly in the scenic climaxes favored by hikers, a fragile country. If man is to blend into the ecosystem, rather than dominate and destroy, he must walk lightly, respectfully, always striving to make his passage through the wilderness invisible.

The public servants entrusted with administration of the region have a complex and difficult job and they desperately need the cooperation of every wildland traveler. Here, the authors would like to express appreciation to these dedicated men and women for their advice on what trips to include in this book and for their detailed review of the text and maps. Thanks are due the Supervisors of the Mt. Baker-Snoqualmie and Wenatchee National Forests, and their district rangers and other staff members.

On behalf of the U.S. Forest Service and The Mountaineers, we invite Americans—and all citizens of Earth—to come and see and live in some of the world's finest wildlands and to vow henceforth to share in the task of preserving the trails and ridges, lakes and rivers, forests and flower gardens for future generations, our children and grandchildren, who will need the wilderness experience at least as much as we do, and probably more.

HELIOTROPE RIDGE

Round trip to Heliotrope Ridge
  6½ miles
Hiking time 5 hours
High point 6000 feet
Elevation gain 2300 feet

Hikable August through
  September
One day or backpack
USGS Mt. Baker

A splendid forest walk leading to a ramble-and-scramble on flowery moraines below (and above) the ice chaos of the rampaging Coleman Glacier. See the mountain climbers—by the hundreds on many summer weekends, because this is the most popular route to the summit of Mt. Baker. They're a harmless and unobtrusive lot, boisterous in camp but sacking out early, rising somber and quiet in the middle of the night, and spending all day on the glaciers, out of sight and sound. Along the trail, hikers can be hugely entertained by the bizarre and colorful displays of tents and axes and ropes and helmets and hardware.

Drive Highway 542 to the town of Glacier and 1 mile beyond to Glacier Creek road, No. 39. Turn right some 8 miles to a parking lot at a sign, "Heliotrope Ridge Trail," elevation 3700 feet.

Hike 2 miles, traversing and switchbacking through tree shadows, over cold little creeks, to the site of Kulshan Cabin, 4700 feet, near but still below timberline. Historic and beloved though it was, the cabin grew old and at last had to be pulled down lest it fall down with somebody inside.

The fun country is above. From the cabin site the trail climbs, crossing several streams which may be gushers from melting snowfields on a hot day. The way passes below steep flower-covered meadows, groves of alpine trees, over a rocky moraine whistling with marmots to another

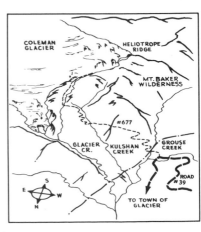

Glacier lilies at edge of snowpatch

Coleman Glacier from trail's end

moraine with a large glacier-scoured rock on the brink of a gravel precipice. Look down to the blue-white jumble of the Coleman Glacier and up to the gleaming ice-capped summit of Mt. Baker. Follow the moraine upward—stopping well short of the living glacier. Good camps below the trail in the timber.

Because of the enormous snowfall on Mt. Baker, and because this is the north side of the mountain, hikers who come earlier than August are liable to be surrounded by snow—and potential danger—above the tree line. The crevasses, of course, are always there, visible or invisible.

Mount Baker from Skyline Ridge

NOOKSACK RIVER
Mount Baker Wilderness

2   SKYLINE DIVIDE

Round trip to knoll 6 miles
Hiking time 4 hours
High point 6215 feet
Elevation gain 1700 feet

Hikable August through
   September
One day or backpack
USGS Mt. Baker

A large, green meadow. An enormous white volcano—pound for pound, the iciest in the Cascades. Views of forests and glaciers, rivers and mountains, sunsets and sunrises.

Drive Highway 542 to 1 mile beyond the town of Glacier. Turn right on Glacier Creek road No. 39 and in a hundred yards turn sharply left on Deadhorse road No. 37. Follow the south side of the Nooksack River some 4 level and pleasant miles. The road then climbs abruptly. At 7½ miles pause to view a lovely waterfall splashing down a rock cleft, coming from the country where you're going. At 13 miles is the parking lot and trailhead, elevation 4500 feet.

The trail, moderate to steep, climbs 2 miles in silver firs and subalpine glades to an immense ridge-top meadow, the beginning of wide views. South are the sprawling glaciers of the north wall of Mt. Baker. North, beyond forests of the Nooksack Valley, are the greenery of Church Mountain and the rock towers of the Border Peaks and, across the border, the Cheam (Lucky Four) Range. On a clear day saltwater can be seen, and the Vancouver Island Mountains, and the British Columbia Coast Range. Eastward is Mt. Shuksan and a gentler companion, little Table Mountain, above Heather Meadows.

The broadest views are atop the 6215-foot knoll to the south; from the meadow, it partly blocks out Baker. Follow the trail ¾ mile along the ridge and take the sidepath up the knoll. Sprawl and enjoy. (Note to photographers: The best pictures of Baker from here generally are taken before 10 a.m. and after 4 p.m.)

Beyond the knoll the trail follows the ridge another ½ mile to a saddle at 6000 feet and then splits. The left contours a scant mile to a dead-end in Chowder Basin, headwaters of Deadhorse Creek, and campsites with all-summer water. The right climbs a step in Skyline Divide to 6500 feet and proceeds along the tundra crest 2 miles to a 6300-foot saddle (and usually, a snowmelt pool) at the foot of the abrupt upward leap of Chowder Ridge, whose summit is accessible on a track suitable for goats, climbers, and life-weary hikers.

In early summer, water is available for camping all along Skyline Divide, but later a party often must look for springs in Chowder and Smith Basins or snowfield dribbles on the ridge.

In benign weather the supreme overnight experience is atop the 6500-foot tundra, watching the Whulj (the name given by the original residents to "the saltwater we know") turn gold in the setting sun and the lights of farms and cities wink on, then awaking at dawn to watch Baker turn shocking pink. However, the tundra is tough enough to withstand sun and frost and storm but not human abuse. Do not build fires; if chilly, crawl in your sleeping bag. Do not sack out on soft turf; lay your sleeping pad and bag on a hard rock or bare dirt.

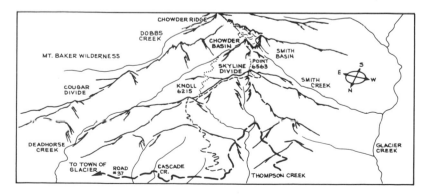

3 CANYON RIDGE

Round trip 6 miles
Hiking time 3 hours
High point 5400 feet
Elevation gain 1200 feet

Hikable August through
September
One day
USGS Mt. Baker

In an area offering so many spectacular viewpoints, why bother hiking to those that rate no better than merely excellent? For one reason, people. On a day when they're swarming all over the spectacular, a per-

Canyon Ridge trail

son may have the excellent all to himself or herself. Also, scenery isn't everything. (In the fog it's nothing.) The forest here is lovely, the flowers bloom by the million, and the heather-and-huckleberry meadows are large and lonesome. Try this trail in early August for the climax of the flower show, or in September when the frost has turned the mountain ash leaves to the color of gold and the blueberry leaves to the color of wine. A party with two cars can do a one-way trip of 8 miles. The description here is a round trip to one of the more excellent views: south to the snowy summits of Church Mountain and the network of logging roads in Canyon Creek valley; north to Canadian mountains and the network of Canadian logging roads.

Drive Highway 542 beyond the town of Glacier 2 miles. Turn left on Canyon Creek road No. 31 and drive 7.2 miles to a junction. For a one-way trip, go left 7 miles on road No. 3140 to the western trailhead, elevation 4500 feet. For the trip described here, stay on road No. 31 and at 14.6 miles from the highway reach the eastern trailhead, elevation 4200 feet.

Start on Damfino trail No. 625, climbing gently through forest. In a long ½ mile turn left on Canyon Ridge trail No. 689. At approximately 1 mile from the road pass Boundary Way trail No. 688. At approximately 1½ miles traverse a large sidehill meadow, steep and unstable, the tread often slumped out. At a long 2 miles the trail crosses Canyon Ridge from the south side to the north and emerges from forest to mountain ash, then heather. The way climbs to a shoulder a few feet from the top of a 5400-foot knob less than 1½ miles from Canada. Excellent enough.

The trail continues another 3 miles to road No. 3140. However, this part of the trail has not been maintained and is best classed as a bushwhack.

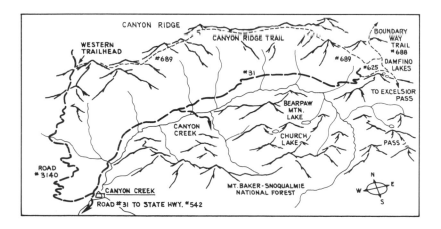

Boundary Way trail

4 POINT 5658

Round trip 6 miles
Hiking time 4 hours
High point 5658 feet
Elevation gain 1500 feet

Hikable late July through
September
One day
USGS Mt. Baker

In the beginning no mountains had names, yet the flowers then were as bright in the meadows and the views to far horizons as inspiring. After the map industry took off, almost everything got a name, needed or not. This one was missed. So was K-2 in the Karakorum. Ponder that as you gaze to panoramas of the North Cascades and whatever, if anything, they call all those mountains in Canada.

Drive 14.6 miles from Highway 542 on Canyon Creek road No. 31 (Hike 3) to the Damfino Lake trailhead, elevation 4200 feet.

Hike Damfino trail No. 625 a long ½ mile and turn left on Canyon Ridge trail No. 689. At approximately 1 mile from the road go right on Boundary Way trail No. 688, through a swampy little cleft, then up in forest to a large meadow. At about 2½ miles from the road attain a 5300-foot ridge top and look across the broad, deep gulf of Tomyhoi Creek into Canada.

The Boundary Way trail goes right, down along the ridge, 2 miles toward—but not to—the border. Don't go. Climb left on the sidepath to the crest of the summit ridge, to an elevation about 3 feet lower than Point 5658. To gain the tippy-top one would have to creep along a knife-edge catwalk. Dogs will prefer to sit down here and chew their bones while enjoying the view north to Canada, west to flatland farm geometry, south to Church Mountain and Mt. Baker, and east to Mt. Shuksan, Tomyhoi, and the garish red masses of the Border Peaks—American Border, Larrabee, and Canadian Border.

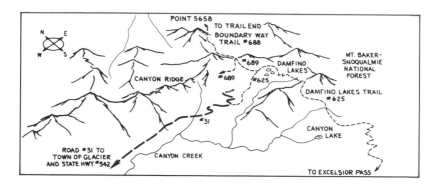

5 EXCELSIOR MOUNTAIN

Round trip from Canyon Creek
road 5½ miles
Hiking time 4 hours
High point 5699 feet
Elevation gain 1500 feet

Hikable mid-July through
September
One day or backpack
USGS Mt. Baker

Views from this meadow summit include Nooksack valley forests and Puget Sound lowlands, Mt. Baker and the Border Peaks, the southernmost portion of the British Columbia Coast Range, and more. Flowers in July, berries and colors in September. Three trails lead to the site of a long-gone lookout cabin; the easiest and most scenic is recommended here, but take your pick.

Drive Highway 542 to the town of Glacier and 2 miles beyond to Canyon Creek road No. 31. Turn left 14.6 miles to the parking lot in a clearcut at the start of trail No. 625; elevation, 4200 feet.

Climb gently through forest ½ mile to the junction with Canyon Ridge trail No. 689 and a bit more to 4500-foot Damfino Lakes, two small ponds surrounded by acres of super-delicious blueberries (in season). Campsites and running water near the smaller lake.

Climb another timbered mile, then go up a narrow draw and shortly enter meadows. Cross a notch, sidehill forest, then broad meadows, rising in ½ mile to 5300-foot Excelsior Pass, some 2½ miles from the road. (Pleasant camps at and near the pass when there is snowfield water—perhaps until early August.) Leave the main trail at the pass and climb a way trail ¼ mile east to the 5699-foot peak.

Sit and look. See the glaciers of Mt. Baker across forests of the Nooksack. See more ice on Mt. Shuksan and other peaks east. See the steepwalled Border Peaks and snowy ranges extending far north into Canada. And see green meadows everywhere.

The summit is a magnificent place to stop overnight in good weather, watching a sunset and a dawn; no water, though, except possible snowmelt.

Two alternate trails can be used to vary the descent. (They can also be used to ascend the peak but for reasons that will be obvious are not the best choices.)

Alternate No. 1: From Excelsior Pass, descend trail No. 670 4 miles and 3500 feet to the highway, reached 8 miles east of Glacier at a small parking area (with trail sign on opposite side of road). The trail switchbacks steeply on south-facing slopes that melt free of snow relatively early in the season; an excellent hike from the highway in May or June, turning back when snowfields halt progress. In summer this route to high country is long and hot and dry.

Alternate No. 2: From the peak traverse High Divide trail No. 630 east 5 miles. At 4960-foot Welcome Pass find a steep trail dropping south 2 miles to an unmaintained logging road; descend the road 2 more miles to the highway, reached at a point some 13 miles east of Glacier. The bottom of this trail also melts free and blossoms out very early.

Experienced off-trail roamers can extend their flower wanders west from Excelsior Pass toward Church Mountain and east from Welcome Pass to Yellow Aster Butte.

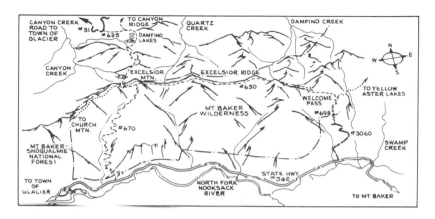

Mount Baker from Excelsior Mountain

Mount Shuksan from side of Church Mountain

NOOKSACK RIVER
Unprotected area

 CHURCH MOUNTAIN

Round trip 8½ miles
Hiking time 6 hours
High point 6100 feet
Elevation gain 4500 feet

Hikable late July through
  September
One day
USGS Mt. Baker

The first thrilling view of emerald meadowland gained while driving
east along Mt. Baker Highway is on Church Mountain. The view is
straight up, nearly a vertical mile, yet the green is so vivid and appears

so close a person cannot but wish to go there. A person can readily do so but must be a sturdy person and carry much water because the climb is far longer than it looks and by midsummer is dry. However, the views back down to the valley and out to Mt. Baker and Shuksan are worth the sweat. In certain kinds of weather the problem is not heat. The viewpoint, on the east peak of Church, is a small platform atop a rocky pinnacle, just large enough to hold the lookout building that used to be here until it was abandoned because wind kept blowing the structure off its foundation.

Drive Highway 542 to the town of Glacier and 7.7 miles beyond. Turn left on road No. 3040, signed "East Church Road." (Avoid the unsigned road at about 7.2 miles.) Drive 2.6 miles to the road-end and trailhead, elevation 1600 feet.

The trail begins on an abandoned logging road, switchbacks up a clearcut to virgin forest, and ascends relentlessly, zigging and zagging. In a bit more than 3 miles the way opens out in heather and flowers and the trail cut can be seen switchbacking up the emerald meadowland to the rocky summit. Shortly below the top is an old storage shed, now a marmot condominium. From here the path, carved from rock, passes an odd-shaped outhouse to the lookout site.

Look down to bugs creeping along the concrete ribbon beside the silver ribbon of river. Look east into the North Cascades, north to Canada, south toward Mt. Rainier. To the west are frightful cliffs of 6315-foot Church Mountain, only 200 feet higher than the lookout peak. Below are the two little Kidney Lakes, snowbound much of the year.

In March and April and May, when the color scheme on high is more white than green, the lower part of the trail offers a fine walk in wildwoods and forest flowers.

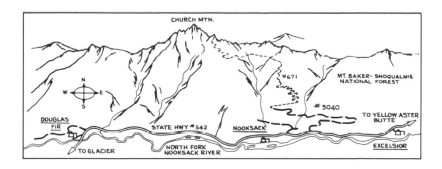

7 YELLOW ASTER BUTTE

Round trip to Yellow Aster Butte
  6 miles
Hiking time 8 hours
High point 6100 feet
Elevation gain 3200 feet

Hikable mid-July through
  October
One day or backpack
USGS Mt. Shuksan

If views turn you on, there's plenty to exclaim about here—across the Nooksack valley to Mt. Baker and Mt. Shuksan, over the headwaters of Tomyhoi Creek to gaudy walls of the Border Peaks, and down to mile-long Tomyhoi Lake and out the valley to farms along the Fraser River. However, many a hiker never bothers to go to the summit of the butte or to lift eyes from the meadows and snowy-cold lakes and ponds set in pockets scooped from the rock by the glacier that appears to have left about a half-hour ago. Try the trip in late July for the flower show, in late August for the blueberry feast, and in October for autumn colors and winter frost.

Drive Highway 542 to Glacier and 13.5 miles beyond to highway maintenance sheds. Just past is a sign, "Tomyhoi Trail 5, Twin Lakes 7." Turn left up narrow, steep, rough road No. 3065 for 2.2 miles then left .2 mile to the Keep Kool Trail No. 699, elevation 2960 feet.

The name, of course, is intended to mock the laboring hiker as he sets out on grown-over logging road of the 1940s, proceeds on straight-up cat track of the same era (high-grading the giant Douglas firs), and continues in virgin forest on a wall-climbing miners' trail, gaining 1200 feet in the first mile. It is nevertheless difficult to get overheated, what with the magnificent deep forest and the creeks to rest by. After the first mile the angle relents and at 4700 feet, about 2 miles, the way flattens to cross a delightful meadow shelf with grand views, bubbling creeks, and superb camps. A steep tilt up through parkland leads to the first tarn at 5200

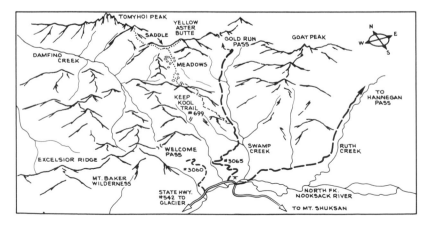

feet, followed in quick succession by more tarns at 5400 feet and the beginning of holes and rusty junk left by the prospectors lest we forget them. At 5500 feet, some 2½ miles, the route (there is now no real trail, nor is one needed) enters the glory hole—a basin with lakes and ponds and pools almost beyond counting. (There are more tucked in pockets up on the ridge.)

An easy stroll leads to the summit of Yellow Aster Butte. A much longer walk climbs from lush herbaceous meadows to tundra to lichen-black felsenmeer very near the summit of 7451-foot Tomyhoi Peak, whose final hundred feet are for climbers only.

Now then: The area having been (largely) given wilderness protection in 1984 the "yellow asters" (actually golden daisies) no longer need the mass support of citizen-hikers or their boots and fires. The crying need is hikers who walk softly, do not build fires in the flowers, and scatter themselves about on the ridge and off in secluded nooks. In summary, particularly tender care for the most beautiful spot on the entire Nooksack Crest.

Goat Mountain from Keep Kool Trail

GOLD RUN PASS— TOMYHOI LAKE

Round trip to Gold Run Pass 4 miles
Hiking time 4 hours
High point 5400 feet
Elevation gain 1800 feet

Hikable July through October
One day or backpack
USGS Mt. Shuksan

Views across the Nooksack valley to Mt. Baker and Mt. Shuksan. Views over the headwaters of Tomyhoi Creek to Tomyhoi Peak and the tall, rough walls of Mt. Larrabee and American Border and Canadian

Mount Shuksan from side of Yellow Aster Butte

Border Peaks. Views down to a mile-long lake and north into Canada. Mountain meadows along a pretty trail—but a hot and dry trail on sunny days, so start early and carry water.

Drive Highway 542 to Glacier and 13.5 miles beyond to highway maintenance sheds. Just past is a sign, "Tomyhoi Trail 5, Twin Lakes 7." Turn left up narrow, steep, rough road No. 3065 for 3 miles, to an intersection; go left. At 4.5 miles is the Tomyhoi Lake trail sign, elevation 3600 feet.

The trail switchbacks steadily up meadows, then trees, then meadows again. In 1½ miles the way leaves forest the last time and enters an open basin, snow-covered until July. South are Baker and a shoulder of Shuksan. Above is Yellow Aster Butte. The display of wildflowers begins here with avalanche lily and spring beauty in mid-June and continues with other species through the summer. At 2 miles is Gold Run Pass, 5400 feet.

Further explorations are inviting. Tomyhoi Lake, 3800 feet, is 2 miles and 1600 feet below the pass. The lake is less than 2 miles from the border; Canadian logging roads can be seen. Avalanche snow floats in the waters until early summer. Good campsite.

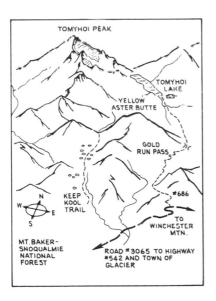

TOMYHOI PEAK

TOMYHOI LAKE

YELLOW ASTER BUTTE

GOLD RUN PASS

KEEP KOOL TRAIL

#686

N W E S

TO WINCHESTER MTN.

MT. BAKER-SNOQUALMIE NATIONAL FOREST

ROAD #3065 TO HIGHWAY #542 AND TOWN OF GLACIER

9 WINCHESTER MOUNTAIN

**Round trip from Twin Lakes 4
 miles
Hiking time 3 hours
High point 6521 feet
Elevation gain 1300 feet
Hikable late July through
 September
One day
USGS Mt. Shuksan**

**Round trip from Tomyhoi
 trailhead 9 miles
Hiking time 6 hours
Elevation gain 3000 feet**

An easy and popular trail through alpine meadows to a summit view of
Baker, Shuksan, Border Peaks, and Tomyhoi, with looks far down to
Tomyhoi Lake and forests of Silesia Creek. Especially beautiful in fall
colors.

Drive Twin Lakes road No. 3065 (Hike 8) 3 miles to an intersection; go
left. At 4.5 miles is the Tomyhoi Lake trail sign, elevation 3600 feet.

The Twin Lakes road is not the work of the Forest Service or built to its

Upper Twin Lake and Canadian peaks

specifications. A "mine-to-market" road, it was constructed by the county and is maintained in the upper reaches solely by the miners, and then only when they are engaged in their sporadic activity, and then only minimally. The first 4.5 miles to the Tomyhoi Lake trail usually are in decent condition, but the final 2.5 miles to Twin Lakes are something else, culminating in five wickedly sharp switchbacks. Many people prefer to protect cars and nerves from damage by parking near the Tomyhoi Lake trail and walking to the lakes. Because road maintenance is so difficult, this last stretch is not open to automobiles until the middle of August, some years not at all; when the miners finally give up, the road will be abandoned, returning Twin Lakes to the realm of trail country—where they belong.

The two lakes, lovely alpine waters at an elevation of 5200 feet, often are frozen until early August, though surrounding parklands melt free earlier. Between the lakes is an undeveloped campsite with a classic view of Mt. Baker.

Find the Winchester Mountain trail at the road end between the lakes. Within ¼ mile is a junction with the High Pass (Gargett Mine) trail. Take the left fork and climb a series of switchbacks westerly through heather, alpine trees, and flowers. Near the top there may be a treacherous snowpatch, steep with no runout, often lasting until late August. It may be possible to squirm between the upper edge of the snow and the rocks. Otherwise, drop below the snow and climb to the trail on the far side. Don't try the snow without an ice ax and experience in using it.

In 1½ miles the trail rounds a shoulder and levels off somewhat for the final ½ mile to the summit, a fine place to while away hours surveying horizons from saltwaterways and lowlands to the Pickets and far north into Canada.

Twin Lakes make a superb basecamp for days of roaming high gardens, prowling old mines, and grazing September blueberries. Even if the upper road must be walked, access is easy for backpacking families with short-legged members.

For one of the longer explorations of the many available, take the High Pass trail (see above). A steep snowfield near the beginning may stop all but trained climbers; if not, there is no further barrier to Low Pass (about 1½ miles) and 5900-foot High Pass (2½ miles). Follow an old miner's trail high on Mt. Larrabee to a close view of the rugged Pleiades. Investigate the junkyard of the Gargett Mine. Wander meadow basins and admire scenery close and distant.

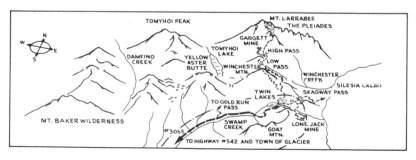

10   NOOKSACK CIRQUE

Round trip to end of gravel bars
  12½ miles
Hiking time 6–8 hours
High point 3100 feet
Elevation gain 600 feet
Hikable August and September

One day or backpack
USGS Mt. Shuksan
Park Service backcountry use
  permit required for camping

A wild, lonesome cirque, one of the most dramatic spots in the North Cascades. Icefalls, waterfalls, rockfalls, moraines, a raging river, the stark pinnacle of Nooksack Tower, and the 5000-foot northeast wall of Mt. Shuksan. But the way is only partly on trail, the rest being bushwhacking and cobble-hopping, and at last report even the trail portion is in terrible shape. The trip can only be recommended to rational people for late summer when the river is low enough to fully expose gravel bars.

Drive Highway 542 east from Glacier 13 miles to the Nooksack River bridge. Just before the bridge, turn left on Nooksack River road No. 32. In 1.3 miles take the right fork, road No. 34, and go another 1 mile to the abandoned bridge over Ruth Creek. Cross the creek and walk 2 miles to the trailhead at the old road-end, elevation about 2550 feet.

The way starts on a grown-over logging road of the 1950s, descending to the right and then climbing, at about 3/4 mile reaching the end of the clearcut and the beginning of true trail, No. 680, at about 2800 feet. Constructed tread goes 1 mile through gorgeous big trees, an old-growth museum, to the end by the river. Cross a large tributary on logs (or an upstream footlog).

For the next ¾ mile there are two alternate ways. Depending on how high the river is and where its channel happens to be, airy and scenic gravel bars may be continuous. Icy Peak appears, then the cirque itself, with hanging ice cliffs of the East Nooksack Glacier falling from Cloudcap (Seahpo) Peak and Jagged Ridge. If the gravel won't go, the woods will. Find the boot-beaten path across some small sloughs, the start marked by a rock cairn. At several places the woods path and the gravel bars are connected by linking paths, permitting alternation.

At the end of this ¾ mile, about 2800 feet, the trail goes out on the gravel for good, a large cairn often marking the spot. The next 1 mile is on gravel bars (which may be under water) or on the riverbank terrace, partly in big timber but mostly in fierce brush, particularly nasty on an enormous alluvial fan issuing from a big gulch.

At the fan-maker creek, 2950 feet, are the last of the big trees. The next ¾ mile is easy, walking mossy gravel on brushfree terraces well above high water.

At 3100 feet, about 4¼ miles from the road, the good times are over and the sensible hiker will make this the turnaround. The view of the cirque, "the deepest, darkest hole in the North Cascades," is superb. The camping (no fires allowed; bring a stove) is splendid.

Upstream from here the river gushes from a virtual tunnel through overhanging alder, with no gravel bars even in the lowest water. If you

Nooksack River and Icy Peak

insist on persisting, dive into the slide alder, watching for cut branches and blazes and cairns. After about 3/4 mile you'll attain the Great Trog (a large rock with an overhang), 3600 feet, formerly the grandest storm camp in the Cascades but now full of boulders. Exploring upward from here is tough going except in spring, when the moraines and cliffs and boulders are buried under fans of avalanche snow, and then it's dangerous.

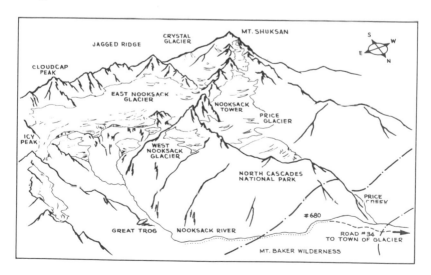

Mount Shuksan from old lookout site on Goat Mountain

11   GOAT MOUNTAIN

Round trip 5 miles
Hiking time 3 hours
High point 4115 feet
Elevation gain 1500 feet

Hikable late June through
   October
One day
USGS Mt. Shuksan (trail
   incorrectly shown)

The views up and down the Nooksack River are glorious. The looks at the ice hanging on the north face of Mt. Shuksan—the West Nooksack Glacier, the Price Glacier, and a lot of little chunks with no names—are stupendous. The viewpoint described here is on the site of a fire-lookout cabin removed in the early 1960s. The trail continues 3 more miles to heather fields, blueberry patches, and campsites at the 6000-foot level of the mountain. The views are at least half again better.

Drive Highway 542 east from Glacier 13 miles. Just before the Nooksack River bridge go left on road No. 32. At 1.5 miles from the highway stay left and at 4 miles find Goat Mountain trail No. 673, elevation 2600 feet.

Presumably the trail was built by miners with tongues hanging out to lap up the pot of gold. The steeper the trail the quicker the riches was the philosophy. At approximately 2 miles the trail briefly flattens, then switchbacks, and about ¼ mile beyond what the USGS maps shows as trail's end, comes to a junction. The main trail proceeds onward and upward 3 miles, as noted above. An unmarked trail turns off right and contours ½ mile to the rocky knoll where the cabin was perched. In addition to valley and glacier views, the highway to Baker Lodge can be seen, the roofs of the recreation area buildings, and all the cars going to and fro, up and down.

Sometimes the trail is hikable to the lookout site in April and May, and then one can see all the yo-yo skiers going to and fro, up and down.

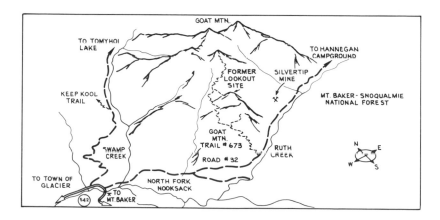

12 HANNEGAN PASS AND PEAK

Round trip to Hannegan Pass 8
miles
Hiking time 6 hours
High point 5066 feet
Elevation gain 2000 feet
Hikable mid-July through
September
One day or backpack
USGS Mt. Shuksan

Round trip to Hannegan Peak 10
miles
Hiking time 8 hours
High point 6186 feet
Elevation gain 3100 feet

A prime entry to the Chilliwack and Picket section of the North Cascades National Park. The walk begins in a delightful valley dominated by the white serenity of Ruth Mountain and concludes with a relaxed wander to a meadow summit offering a panorama of the north wall of Shuksan, the Pickets, and wildness high and low.

Drive Highway 542 east from Glacier 13 miles to the Nooksack River bridge. Just before the bridge turn left on Nooksack River road No. 32. In about 1.5 miles take the left fork, Ruth Creek road No. 32 and continue 4.5 miles to road-end at Hannegan Campground, 3000 feet.

The first trail mile ascends gently through trees and avalanche-path greenery near Ruth Creek, with looks upward to the waterfall-streaked cliffs and pocket icefields of Mt. Sefrit and Nooksack (Ruth) Ridge. At a bit more than 1 mile the snow dome of Ruth Mountain comes in sight—a startling expanse of whiteness for so small a peak. Now the path steepens, climbing above the valley floor.

Rest stops grow long, there is so much to see. At 3½ miles, 4600 feet, trail swings to the forest edge beside a meadow-babbling creek; across the creek is a parkland of heather benches and alpine trees. Splendid campsites, the best on the route; those least harmful to the terrain are designated by the Forest Service, which wishes campers would not build fires here. The final ½ mile switchbacks in forest to Hannegan Pass, 5066 feet.

Views from the pass are restricted by trees; the camping is so poor (scarce wood, undependable water) and so damaging to the tiny meadow it is strongly discouraged and ought to be forbidden. Hikers who come only to the pass will feel richly rewarded by scenes along the way but may be disappointed by the lack of a climactic vista. A sidetrip is therefore recommended.

Visitors usually are drawn southward and upward on the climbers' track toward Ruth Mountain. This path leads to lovely meadows and broader views but dwindles to nothing before long, tempting the unwary onto steep and dangerous snow slopes. Leave Ruth to the climbers. There's a better and safer sidetrip.

From the pass, saunter westerly up open forest, following game traces when available. Emerge into a steep, lush meadow (slippery when wet), at the top break through a screen of trees to heather and flowers, and wander wide-eyed up the crest of a rounded ridge to the summit plateau of Hannegan Peak, 6186 feet. Roam the meadow flats, looking down into valley forests of Ruth and Silesia Creeks and Chilliwack River, looking out to glaciers and cliffs of Baker, Shuksan, Ruth, Triumph, Challenger, Redoubt, Slesse, and dozens of other grand peaks.

In good weather a party can camp comfortably on the summit; carry a stove for cooking, collect water from snowfield trickles and enjoy the panorama in sunset and dawn.

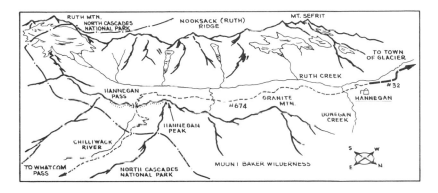

Looking north from side of Hannegan Peak

13 COPPER MOUNTAIN

Round trip to Copper Mountain
  Lookout 20 miles
Allow 2–3 days
High point 6260 feet
Elevation gain about 4800 feet in,
  1500 feet out

Hikable August through
  September
USGS Mt. Shuksan and Mt.
  Challenger
Park Service backcountry use
  permit required for camping

A remote meadow ridge on the west edge of the North Cascades National Park, offering a rare combination of easy-walking terrain and panoramas of rough-and-cold wilderness. Views across far-below forests of the Chilliwack River to the Picket Range—and views west to other superb peaks and valleys. However, hikers planning a visit should be aware of restrictions on use of the area. The Park Service currently permits use of only eleven campsites on the entire 6-mile length of the ridge. A water shortage is said to be the limiting factor. Hikers who plan trips for midweek generally will have no trouble obtaining a site. No fires allowed anywhere; carry a stove.

Drive to Hannegan Campground and hike 4 miles, gaining 2000 feet, to Hannegan Pass (Hike 12). Descend forest switchbacks into avalanche-swept headwaters of the Chilliwack River, then sidehill along talus and stream outwash patched with grass and flowers. Note chunks of volcanic breccia in the debris and look up to their source in colorful cliffs—remnants of ancient volcanoes.

At 1 mile and 650 feet below Hannegan Pass is a 4400-foot junction and a nice riverside campsite, Boundary Camp. The Chilliwack River trail goes right, descending. The Copper Mountain trail goes left and up, entering forest and climbing steadily, switchbacking some, crossing the upper portion of Hells Gorge (sliced into volcanic rocks), and emerging into parkland.

At 7 miles the trail attains the 5500-foot ridge crest between Silesia Creek and the Chilliwack River. A memorable look back to Hannegan Pass, Ruth Mountain, and Shuksan—and the beginning of miles of constant views.

The trail continues along the open crest, up a bit and down a bit, then climbs around a knob to a wide, grassy swale at 8 miles. Some 300 feet and a few minutes below the swale is little Egg Lake, 5200 feet, set in rocks and flowers. Three legal campsites are at the lake, two others on Knob 5689, Silesia Camp.

The way goes up and down another knob to a broad meadow at 9 miles. Now comes the final mile, gaining 1100 feet to 6260-foot Copper Mountain Lookout, the climax. Beyond the green deeps of Silesia Creek are the Border Peaks and the incredible fang of Slesse—and far-off in haze, ice giants of the British Columbia Coast Range. Look down and down to the white thread of the Chilliwack River and beyond its forest valley to Redoubt and Bear and Indian and the magnificent Pickets. Also see Shuksan and Baker. And more peaks and streams, an infinity of wildland.

Mount Shuksan from Copper Ridge

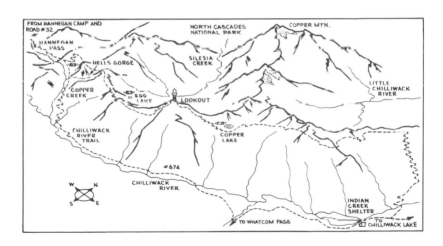

Beyond the lookout the trail descends about 1½ miles to the three campsites at 5200-foot Copper Lake (blue waters under steep cliffs), then traverses and descends about 7 more miles (views much of the way) to the Chilliwack River trail at 2300 feet; this junction is 15 miles from Hannegan Pass. A 34-mile loop trip using this return route adds low-valley forests to the high-ridge wander.

For another exploration leave the trail before the steep descent to Copper Lake and investigate ridges and basins toward the 7142-foot summit of Copper Mountain.

14   EASY RIDGE

Round trip 27 miles
Allow 3 days
High point 6100 feet
Elevation gain 5500 feet in, 2400
   feet out

Hikable late July through
   September
USGS Mt. Shuksan and Mt.
   Challenger
Park Service backcountry use
   permit required for camping

A not-so-easy trail to a high green ridge surrounded by rugged and icy peaks. Wander amid picturesque alpine trees, fields of flowers, and small tarns, admiring the Chilliwack wilderness of the North Cascades National Park. The difficulty of the trip is compensated for by the privacy—and the views.

Drive to Hannegan Campground and hike 4 miles, gaining 2000 feet, to Hannegan Pass (Hike 12). Descend the Chilliwack River trail, dropping 2300 feet in 5½ miles. At 9½ miles, elevation 2800 feet, is the Easy Ridge trail junction. Go right, reaching a ford of the Chilliwack River in about ¼ mile. Except perhaps in late summer the river is too deep, swift, and cold to ford and a log must be found. Usually one is available within

Crossing Chilliwack River

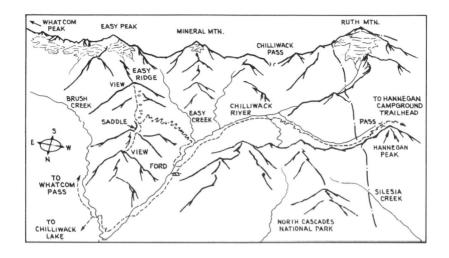

¼ mile of the ford, upstream or down. Give preference to searching upstream, since on the far side the trail parallels the river about ¼ mile before heading uphill along Easy Creek. If luck is bad in this direction, logs are generally abundant ½ mile downstream, by the U.S. Cabin Camp; in this case the trail can be regained without too much brush-beating if one stays near or on the valley wall. A good plan is to camp the first night by the ford, locating a footlog that evening for use the next morning.

The trail was built to a Forest Service fire-lookout cabin, long since demolished. The Park Service maintains the tread for "resource protection," a college-educated term meaning the fallen trees are cut out and water drained off. That's good enough, brush being no problem. The hillside forest is entirely dry so fill canteens at the bottom. Or use the old mountain trick of sucking a prune seed.

The trail switchbacks steeply 2.6 miles, gaining 2600 feet, to the first views at a 5200-foot saddle in Easy Ridge. From the saddle the trail continues north ½ mile to the old lookout site on a 5640-foot knoll overlooking the junction of Brush Creek and the Chilliwack River; great looks down into valleys, across to the pleasant ridge of Copper Mountain, and off to rough, white peaks. For the broadest views leave the trail at the saddle and walk the main ridge south, climbing open slopes, past a number of tarns, to a heather-covered knoll at 6100 feet. A tiny pool here, good for cold drinks while looking at Shuksan and icy west, Canadian peaks north, Redoubt northeast, Whatcom Peak close by to the east, and mountains and valleys beyond number.

The route to the 6613-foot summit of Easy Peak may be blocked by a steep snow slope—don't try it without an ice ax and knowledge of self-arrest technique. The view from the top isn't much better than from the heather knoll.

For a 3-day trip the best camp is on a gravel bar at the Chilliwack River ford. For longer trips, allowing more time to explore highlands, carry packs to wonderful camps near the small tarns. Camp only on bare ground or snow. No fires.

15 WHATCOM PASS

Round trip 34 miles
Allow 3–5 days
High point 5200 feet
Elevation gain 4600 feet in, 2600
    feet out

Hikable late July through
    September
USGS Mt. Shuksan and Mt.
    Challenger
Park Service backcountry use
    permit required for camping

A long hike on an old miners' route to the Caribou goldfields in Canada, entering the heart of the most spectacular wilderness remaining in the contiguous 48 states. Virgin forests in a U-shaped valley carved by ancient glaciers; rushing rivers; mountain meadows; and a sidetrip to lovely Tapto Lakes, the ultimate blend of gentle beauty and rough grandeur. Whatcom Pass is the high point on the walk across the North Cascades National Park from the Mt. Baker region to Ross Lake, in recent years recognized as a classic of the American wildlands.

Drive to Hannegan Campground and hike 4 miles, gaining 2000 feet, to Hannegan Pass (Hike 12). Descend the Chilliwack River trail, which drops rapidly at first and then gentles out in delightful forest, reaching U.S. Cabin Camp at 10 miles.

At about 11 miles, elevation 2468 feet (2600 feet down from Hannegan Pass), the trail crosses the Chilliwack River on a cablecar. The way now climbs moderately to the crossing of Brush Creek at about 12 miles. Here is a junction.

The Chilliwack trail goes north 9 miles to the Canadian border and about 1 mile more to Chilliwack Lake. The forest walk to the border is worth taking in its own right; parties visiting the region during early summer when the high country is full of snow may prefer pleasures of the low, green world. (See note on border crossing in Hike 100.)

From the 2600-foot junction the Brush Creek trail climbs steadily, gaining 2600 feet in the 5 miles to Whatcom Pass. At 13 miles is Graybeal Camp (hikers and horses), at 15 miles Tapto Camp, at 16½ miles the two sites of Whatcom Camp (no fires), and at 17 miles 5200-foot Whatcom Pass.

Views from the meadowy pass are superb but there is vastly more to

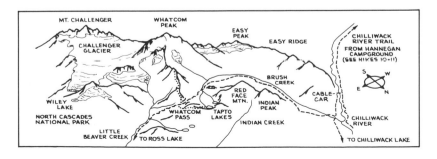

Mount Challenger from Whatcom Pass

see. The first thing to do is ramble the easy ridge south of the pass to a knoll overlooking the boggling gleam of Challenger Glacier. Tapto Lakes are next. Climb steep slopes north from the pass, following a boot-built path in alpine forest. When the hillside levels off continue left in meadows to rocky ground above the lakes. Enjoy the waters and flowers, the stupendous view of Challenger.

In addition to the on-trail camps, cross-country, no-fire camping is permitted at Tapto Lakes and on Whatcom Arm. There is *no* camping at Whatcom Pass.

The "across the national park" hike from Hannegan Campground to Big Beaver Landing on Ross Lake covers 38½ up-and-down miles on easy trail beside wild rivers, through gorgeous forests, over three passes. Total elevation gain on the way, 5400 feet. To have time for sidetrips a party should allow 7–9 days. From Whatcom Pass drop abruptly (56 switchbacks!) into headwaters of Little Beaver Creek, an enchanting place where waterfalls tumble from cliffs all around. Camping here at Twin Rocks Camp, 3000 feet. At 6 miles from Whatcom Pass is Stillwell Camp and the 2400-foot junction with the Beaver Pass trail. To conclude the cross-park journey, see Hike 33.

16   LAKE ANN

Round trip to Lake Ann 8 miles
Hiking time 6–8 hours
High point (at the saddle) 4800 feet
Elevation gain about 1000 feet in,
   1000 feet out

Hikable August through
   September
One day or backpack
USGS Mt. Shuksan

When North Cascades climbers and hikers compare memories of favorite sitting-and-looking places, Lake Ann always gets fond mention. The Mt. Shuksan seen from here is quite different from the world-famous roadside view, yet the 4500-foot rise of glaciers and cliffs is at least as grand. And there is plenty to do. However, if taking the trip on a

Curtis Glacier and Mount Shuksan from Lake Ann

weekend, make it a day hike—you'll be hard-pressed to find an empty campsite.

Drive highway 542 to the Mt. Baker ski area. Continue on gravel road about 1½ miles upward to the parking lot at Austin Pass, 4700 feet. Until August, snow blocks the road somewhere along the way, adding ½ mile or so of walking.

The trail begins by dropping 600 feet to a delightful headwater basin of Swift Creek. Brooks meander in grass and flowers. Marmots whistle from boulder-top perches. Pleasant picnicking.

From the basin the trail descends a bit more and traverses forest, swinging around the upper drainage of Swift Creek. At 2¼ miles is the lowest elevation (3900 feet) of the trip, an attractive camp in meadows by a rushing stream, and a junction with the Swift Creek trail. If camping beyond here, carry a stove; the era of building fires at and near the lake is long past.

Now starts a 900-foot ascent in 1½ miles, first in heather and clumps of Christmas trees, then over a granite rockslide into forest under a cliff, to a cold and open little valley. If the way is snow-covered, as it may be until mid-August, plod onward and upward to the obvious 4800-foot saddle, beyond which is Lake Ann. When whiteness melts away, the waterfalls and moraines and flowers and ice-plucked buttresses of the little valley demand a slow pace.

What to do next? First off, sit and watch the living wall of Shuksan. Then, perhaps, circumnavigate the lake, noting the contact between granitic rocks and complex metamorphics. In September, blueberry upward on the ridge of Mt. Ann. If time allows, go on longer wanders.

Recommended Wander No. 1: Follow the trail from Lake Ann as it dips into the headwater basin of Shuksan Creek, then switchbacks up and up toward Shuksan. At a rocky gully a climber's track branches steeply to the left. Just here the main trail may be nonexistent for a few yards; if so, scramble across gravel to regain the tread. Continue to a promontory a stone's throw from the snout of the Lower Curtis Glacier. Look up to ,the mountain. Look down forests to Baker Lake. Look beyond Swift Creek to the stupendous whiteness of Mt. Baker.

Recommended Wander No. 2: From the Lake Ann saddle climb the heathery spur to Shuksan Arm, with spectacular campsites (snowbanks for water) and views both of Baker and Shuksan.

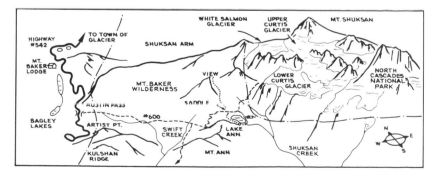

Mount Baker reflected in Iceberg Lake

NOOKSACK RIVER
Partly in Mount Baker Wilderness

17   CHAIN LAKES LOOP

Round trip 6 miles
Hiking time 4 hours
High point 5400 feet
Elevation gain 1500 feet

Hikable late July through
   October
One day
USGS Mt. Shuksan

Alpine meadows loaded with blueberries (in season), a half-dozen small lakes, and at every turn of the trail a changing view, dominated by "the magnificent pair," the white volcano of Mt. Baker and the massive architecture of Mt. Shuksan. The area is a wildlife sanctuary, so deer and goat are frequently seen. All this on an easy hike circling the base of a high plateau guarded on every side by impressive lava cliffs.

Drive Highway 542 to closed-in-summer Mt. Baker Lodge (Heather Meadows Recreation Area). Continue on gravel road 3 miles upward to the 5200-foot road-end on Kulshan Ridge. The winter snowpack here is often 25 feet deep on the level, with much greater depths in drifts, so the road commonly is snowbound until late August. Drive as far as possible and walk the rest of the way.

Because the trailhead often is buried in deep snow until September, many hikers start on the wrong path. Look on the Mt. Baker side of the road-end Artist Point parking lot and spot the big, wide trail dropping a short way into forest. (Don't make the mistake of going uphill, toward Table Mountain—unless, of course, that's where you *want* to go.)

(The Table Mountain trail climbs 500 feet through lava cliffs to grand views atop the plateau; to here, the walk is easy and rewarding. The trail then continues over Table Mountain and descends cliffs to meet the Chain Lakes trail. However, on the way it crosses a steep and dangerous snowfield which has killed enough hikers that the summit traverse is not recommended.)

The Chain Lakes trail traverses almost on the level a short mile around the south side of Table Mountain to a saddle between Table Mountain and Ptarmigan Ridge. At the junction here take the right fork, dropping 300 feet to the first of the four Chain Lakes, tiny Mazama Lake, reached about 1¾ miles from the road. A bit beyond is aptly named Iceberg Lake, which many years never melts out completely. Halfway around the shore, see Hayes Lake on the left. A sidetrail follows the Hayes Lake shore and crosses a low rise to Arbuthnot Lake. Don't try to push the route farther; return the way you came.

The main trail now begins a 600-foot climb to 5400-foot Herman Saddle at about 3 miles. Cliffs of the narrow slot frame Baker west, Shuksan east. Spend some time sitting and looking from one to the other. Then descend amid boulders, heather, and waterfalls, dropping 1100 feet to meadow-surrounded Bagley Lakes. Pause to wander flower fields of the inlet stream. Look for skiers on the north side of Table Mountain; die-hards ski the permanent snowfields all summer and fall, until winter sends them to other slopes.

Between the Bagley Lakes find an unmaintained path (easy going even if the tread is lost) climbing to the Austin Pass Warming Hut and the Artist Point parking area, gaining 900 feet in 2 miles. If transportation can be arranged (by use of two cars or a helpful friend), this final ascent can be eliminated.

Iceberg on Iceberg Lake

18 PTARMIGAN RIDGE

Round trip to Camp Kiser about 8 miles
Hiking time 8 hours
High point 6000 feet

Hikable August through September
One day or backpack
USGS Mt. Baker and Mt. Shuksan

Begin in meadows, climb a bit to the snowy and rocky crest of a ridge open to the sky, and wander for miles on the high line toward the lofty white mass of Mt. Baker. This hike has no single destination; a party may go a short way until stopped by snow, or continue a long way to close-up views of the splendid Rainbow Glacier, or accept the invitation of sidetrips. Everything is purely delightful.

Keep in mind, though, that Ptarmigan Ridge is basically "climbers' country." In late summer of light-snowfall years, in good weather, hikers can venture into the wild and lonesome highland, but even then they must be well-equipped and experienced.

Drive to Kulshan Ridge road-end at 5200 feet and hike 1 mile to the saddle between Table Mountain and Ptarmigan Ridge (Hike 17). At the junction take the left fork, Camp Kiser trail No. 683. The trail drops a bit and then climbs around the side of the 5628-foot hump marking the north end of Ptarmigan Ridge. Snowfields often linger here through the summer and may force casual walkers to turn back.

Beyond the hump the trail climbs (often on snow) to a ridge crest and traverses some 2½ miles to Camp Kiser. The tread is sketchy, snow crossings may be frequent, and the route becomes increasingly difficult

Ptarmigan in summer plumage

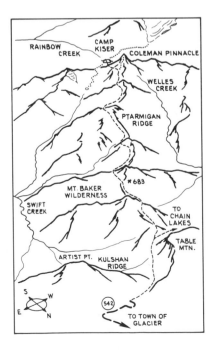

to follow and increasingly easy to lose, despite rock cairns. In fog, even skilled alpine navigators get confused; spur ridges may be mistaken for the main ridge and lead a party far astray.

The Baker-Shuksan scenery is steadily dazzling and off-trail tours of high rocks and waterfall-loud basins are constantly tempting. Listen to marmots and conies whistling and squeaking. Watch for goats. And ptarmigan.

The trail swings around the south side of 6414-foot Coleman Pinnacle to Camp Kiser, which is not a specific place but rather a ½-mile stretch of ridgeslope benches sprinkled with mountain hemlock. Though this route to the summit of Mt. Baker is not popular, here is where the occasional climbers camp.

Camp Kiser offers many fine spots to stop overnight or longer. Water is plentiful but not wood; carry a stove. The place cries out for a basecamp to enjoy the explorations. Walk to near the top of Coleman Pinnacle—and scramble to the summit if competent to do so. Wander the climber's track another mile or two closer to the glaciers. Or drop 500 feet down meadows to the cold little basin southeast of Coleman Pinnacle, only recently evacuated by a glacier, remnants of which linger; roam the shores of a newborn, ice-fed lakelet.

Mount Baker from Camp Kiser

ELBOW LAKE

Round trip 6 miles
Hiking time 4 hours
High point 3400 feet
Elevation gain 1300 feet

Hikable mid-July through
  October
One day or backpack
USGS Hamilton

Three (well, really two and a half) forest-ringed lakes in a narrow cleft of Sister Divide. Come alone and you'll find peace and quiet. However, you'll hardly ever find a time to be alone because of the throngs of fisher-

Fungus near Elbow Lake

men looking for fresh meat and the families looking for a picnic or an easy backpack. Relax and enjoy the gleeful shouts and happy laughter; no red-blooded youngster can communicate in anything less than a yell, preferably loud enough to carry across a lake and up a mountain.

The shortest approach is from the south on a 1½-mile trail ideal for tiny hikers on their first outing. Drive to the end of road No. 12, elevation 3000 feet, ½ mile from Baker Pass trail No. 603. (See Hike 21 for driving directions.) The trail gains only 400 feet, practically flat.

For the approach described here and recommended as most interesting, drive Highway 9 from Sedro Woolley toward Sumas. At the hamlet of Acme cross the South Fork Nooksack River and turn off on Mosquito Lake road. At 9.5 miles from the highway, just before crossing Porter Creek, go right on road No. 38 for another 11 miles to trail No. 697, elevation 2100 feet.

Begin by descending toward the river on an old road become a trail. Skirt a swampy area, head several hundred feet upriver to the end of an old clearcut, and look for a faint trail on the right. Beat through the brush, never daunted, to a substantial bridge.

The trail follows the Middle Fork Nooksack River downstream ½ mile and abruptly turns south for a steady ascent along Green Creek. At 2 miles the forest briefly opens for a view up the valley to the reddish rock of Twin Sisters and Skookum Peak. Back in the deep woods, the way parallels Hildebrand Creek, which goes dry in late summer.

At 2¾ miles, 3350 feet, is small, marshy Lake (half a lake) Hildebrand. Continue ¼ mile to much larger Elbow Lake, 3400 feet, with several small but comfortable campsites. From the far shore climb a small rise to Lake Doreen, boxed in by steep hillsides that make camping tortuous.

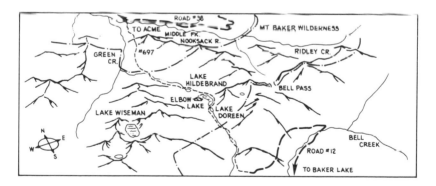

20
PARK BUTTE— RAILROAD GRADE

Round trip to Park Butte 7 miles
Hiking time 6–8 hours
High point 5450 feet
Elevation gain 2250 feet

Hikable mid-July through
  October
One day or backpack
USGS Hamilton and Mt. Baker

Recommending any one hike in the parklands of Mt. Baker's southwest flank is like praising a single painting in a museum of masterpieces. There are days of wandering here, exploring meadows and moraines, waterfalls and lakes, listening to marmots and watching for mountain goats. The trail to Morovitz Meadow gives a good sampling of the country, with impressive near views of the glaciers of Baker, the towering Black Buttes (core of an ancient volcano), the Twin Sisters, and far horizons.

Drive Highway 20 east from Sedro Woolley 14.5 miles and turn left on the Baker Lake—Grandy Lake road. In 12.5 miles, just past Rocky Creek bridge, turn left on Loomis—Nooksack road No. 12, go 3 miles to Sulphur Creek road No. 13, and follow it 6 miles to the end in a logging patch at about 3200 feet. Find the trail west of the road, near Sulphur Creek.

The trail immediately crosses Sulphur Creek into the heather and blueberries (in season) of Schreibers Meadow, passes frog ponds and a dilapidated shelter cabin, then enters forest. In 1 mile is an interesting area where meltwater from the Easton Glacier has torn wide avenues through the trees. The drainage pattern changes from time to time; generally three torrents must be crossed by footlog or boulder-hopping.

Beyond the boulder-and-gravel area the trail enters cool forest and switchbacks steeply a long mile to lower Morovitz Meadow. The grade gentles in heather fields leading to upper Morovitz Meadow, 4500 feet. Pleasant campsites here, some in alpine trees, some in open gardens beside snowmelt streams. Please do not build fires; carry a stove.

Snout of Easton Glacier

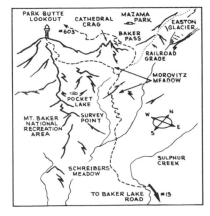

62

Mount Baker lost in clouds from Park Butte trail

At the trail junction in the upper meadow, go left to Park Butte, climbing to a ridge and in a mile reaching the 5450-foot summit. Views of Mt. Baker glaciers (and much more) are magnificent. Parties with spare time and energy may well be tempted to descend to the delightful basin of Pocket Lake or roam the ridge to 6100-foot Survey Point.

There is another direction to go from Morovitz Meadow. Leave the trail near the junction and ramble upward to the intriguing crest of Railroad Grade, a moraine built by the Easton Glacier in more ambitious days. Look down the unstable wall of gravel and boulders to the naked wasteland below the ice. Walk the narrow crest higher and yet higher, closer and closer to the gleaming volcano. In late summer hikers can scramble moraine rubble and polished slabs to about 7000 feet before being forced to halt at the edge of the glacier.

From either Railroad Grade or Baker Pass, inventive walkers can pick private ways through waterfall-and-flower country to the edge of a startling chasm. Look down to the chaotic front of the Deming Glacier, across to stark walls of the Black Buttes. All through the wide sprawl of Mazama Park are secluded campsites, beauty spots to explore. Don't forget Little Mazama Lake or nearby Meadow Point.

Mount Baker from Baker Pass trail

BAKER RIVER
Unprotected area

 BAKER PASS

Round trip 10 miles
Hiking time 6 hours
High point 4964 feet
Elevation gain 2000 feet

Hikable mid-July through
   October
One day or backpack
USGS Hamilton

A little-used trail skims ridges and roams meadows to touch the very edge of the mighty glaciers on the south side of Mt. Baker. Why so little use? Because there's a much shorter approach via Schreibers Meadow

(Hike 20). But why be in such a rush all the time? Half the fun of a hike is the getting there. The longer the trail, the more the fun. However, don't do this one until July 1; before that the entire upper valley of the South Fork Nooksack River is restricted, and the road gated, to let cow elks drop their calves undisturbed.

Drive the Baker Lake—Grandy Lake road and turn onto the Loomis-Nooksack road No. 12 (Hike 20). In 3.5 miles go left staying on road No. 12 for another 15 miles to Baker Pass trail No. 603, elevation 3400 feet.

Thin tread ascends dense—and as of this writing not yet clearcut—forest, leveling off somewhat after a first steep push. At 2 miles the trail crosses the Sister Divide from the south to the north side at Bell Pass, 3962 feet. Views extend west to the Twin Sisters Range, north over the chainsaw massacre of the Middle Fork Nooksack River, and east to the gigantic dazzlement of Mt. Baker.

At 3 miles overlook Ridley Creek, then traverse beneath massive cliffs below Park Butte Lookout and into the beautiful meadows of Mazama Park. Here is the officially designated camping area for the Park Butte vicinity, at and around the junction with Ridley Creek trail No. 690, 4400 feet.

The trail climbs steeply a final ½ mile, rounding rocky Cathedral Crag and switchbacking to the narrow slot of Baker Pass, 4964 feet. Way trails lead to Railroad Grade, as the lateral moraine of Easton Glacier is called, for climax views of volcano, crater (perhaps steaming), and a world composed solely of snow and ice.

Loopers in the mood for a 12-mile day or backpack can descend the Ridley Creek trail to a shaky and possibly transient log crossing of the Middle Fork Nooksack River. (On hot days the river rolls over the top of the log; be prepared to bivouac, in hopes of a cold night.) Across the river is road No. 38, which in 1½ miles reaches Elbow Lake trail No. 697 (Hike 19). Follow it over the Sister Divide at Lake Doreen and return to road No. 12 at ½ mile from the Baker Pass trail.

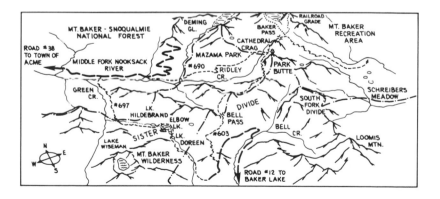

22 BOULDER RIDGE

Round trip 8 miles
Hiking time 7 hours
High point 4500 feet
Elevation gain 1300 feet

Hikable July through October
One day or backpack
USGS Mt. Baker

A rough hike to one of the many beautiful alpine ridges radiating like octopus arms from the white heap of Mount Baker. The crest provides a magnificent overlook of the Boulder Glacier.

Drive Highway 20 east from Sedro Woolley 14½ miles. Turn left on the Baker Lake-Grandy Lake road 14 miles to Komo Kulshan Guard Station and continue 4 miles to the Boulder Creek bridge. About ¼ mile beyond, turn left on Marten Lake road No. 1131. In 2 miles stay left again and drive 3½ more miles to the road-end and trailhead, elevation 3200 feet.

The trail contours up and down, going through bogs and waist-high huckleberry bushes, gaining only 300 feet in 2 miles. Then, ¼ mile after crossing a little stream, the tread vanishes in a small, marshy meadow; no formal trail ever existed beyond here. At the far end of the meadow is an obscure blaze and the start of a very faint climbers' path angling to the right toward the ridge crest. Follow the blazes and plastic ribbons carefully. The track is steep, sometimes among evergreen trees and occasionally through slide alder. After climbing some 500 feet above the meadow, the way bursts from timber onto a moraine covered with knee-high firs and hemlocks.

From here there is a choice: an easy ¾-mile hike, the route obvious, to the top of the moraine and a close view of Boulder Glacier; or, an ascent of 500 feet in 1 mile to Boulder Ridge.

Weather-exposed but scenic camps are possible on the ridge; plan to cook on a stove and find meager water from snowfields, if any.

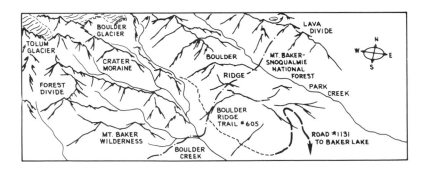

Mount Baker from Boulder Ridge trail

23   RAINBOW RIDGE

Round trip 4½ miles
Hiking time 3 hours
High point 4800 feet
Elevation gain 1200 feet plus ups
  and downs

Hikable August through mid-
  September
One day
USGS Mt. Shuksan

The meadows are simply grand, the looks down down down to Avalanche Gorge are awesome, and the views of the spectacular south face of Mt. Shuksan across the valley and the crevasses of the Park Glacier close

Snout of Rainbow Glacier from Rainbow Ridge

at hand can be a mystical experience. Moreover, the path was built solely by boots, isn't shown on maps and is barely visible on the ground, so the chances of solitude are much better than on the average Mt. Baker trail. Drive Highway 20 to the Baker Lake-Grandy Lake road and turn north 18 miles, to just beyond the Boulder Creek bridge. Turn left on road No. 1130 for 9.4 miles, to the end in a clearcut, elevation 3600 feet.

The boot-beaten path, easy to lose, weaves around trees and over logs, through waist-high huckleberry bushes. If you lose it, don't play guessing games—stop and backtrack to the last spot the trail was definite and try again. The way gains 800 feet in the first mile, to a small meadow with a tantalizing glimpse of Mt. Baker. In the next ¼ mile it gains 250 feet to meadows on the crest of Rainbow Ridge, 4400 feet, and views across the gulf of Swift Creek to the towers of Mt. Shuksan.

In fields of heather and alpine blueberries, alternating between views of Mt. Shuksan and Mt. Baker, the trail rides the ups and downs of the ridge crest to a 4800-foot high point. This is a great place to call it quits, to get out the watermelon and the freeze-dried pizza, to gaze a vertical 2000 feet down into Avalanche Gorge, to admire the snout of the Rainbow Glacier. The trail fades on the way to the next high point, then vanishes; one suspects the construction hereabouts was less by boots than goat feet.

Camps atop the ridge are sensational, watching the rosy sunset on Shuksan's cliffs and the pink sunrise on Baker's glacier. However, the only water is from snowbanks, if any. So carry *two* watermelons. Either that or have supper at the car, hike to the ridge in twilight, and return to the car for breakfast. Camp near the trail so that if a low cloud slips in by night you can find the way down. The vicinity of a 2000-foot cliff is no place to be searching for goat tracks in the fog.

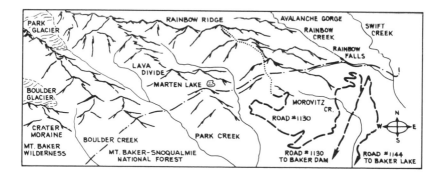

SWIFT CREEK

Round trip 4 miles
Hiking time 3 hours
High point 1600 feet
Elevation gain 800 feet in, 300 feet
  out

Hikable May through October
One day or backpack
USGS Mt. Shuksan

Once upon a time, in days not so olden but that some folks still on the trails don't remember them fondly, the 10-mile trail from Baker Lake to Austin Pass was a major thoroughfare heavily trampled by the Old Rangers, the dirty miners in search of shining gold, and assorted bushwhackers. Nowadays, of course, the parking lot at Austin Pass is generally considered such small satisfaction for walking 10 uphill miles that the route is traveled the whole way mainly by fanatics who take joy in the fact the trail has been, in effect, abandoned by the Forest Service and let go back to nature.

However, the lower stretch of the trail offers so delightful a walk through magnificently virgin forest as to be extremely popular. It would be more so were the Forest Service to courageously confront Rainbow Creek, a raging glacial torrent that changes course every year or two, and do such engineering as would permit the route to dependably cross and proceed into the Mount Baker Wilderness.

From Highway 20 drive Baker Lake-Grandy Lake road 19.7 miles, to just opposite the entrance to Baker Lake Resort. Turn left on road No. 1144 for 3 miles to Swift Creek trail No. 607, elevation 1200 feet.

The trail drops some 200 feet in ½ mile through marvelous old forest to Rainbow Creek. If a logjam exists, proceed. If not, take a very slow pace back the ½ mile, the more fully to absorb the good juices from the primeval scene; the torrent is much too swift to wade, as is necessary to get to Swift Creek.

On the far side the trail follows within sound of Rainbow Creek, whose mists nourish the moss carpet of the forest floor, and in about ¾ mile enters Mount Baker Wilderness. After ¼ mile of minor ups and downs it switchbacks up 300 feet in ½ mile, then levels off and plunges into brush as high as a tall hiker's eye. The tread is as easy to find at night as in day; feet have to do it.

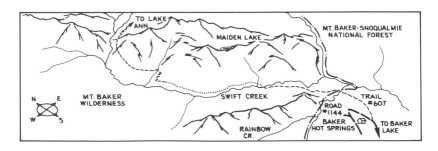

Crossing Rainbow Creek on a logjam

At 2 miles, 1600 feet, the way touches the bank of Swift Creek. In early summer when the mountain's snow is being flushed back to the oceans to recharge them for the next winter's storms, the "creek" is a raging river. By midsummer, though, it has quieted to a delicious stream of clear, cool water, with gravel bars that cry out to be camped on.

Mount Baker from Shannon Ridge

SHANNON RIDGE

Round trip 6 miles
Hiking time 4 hours
High point 4700 feet
Elevation gain 2200 feet

Hikable July through September
One day
USGS Mt. Shuksan

Heather-covered Shannon Ridge gives the really big picture of Mt. Baker, lofting high above the canyon depths of Swift and Shuksan Creeks, and the champion views across Baker Lake (reservoir) to glaciers on Hagan Mountain and Mt. Blum. Getting there demands much blood in fly time, a lot of sweat on hot days, and occasionally a fair number of tears.

Drive from Highway 20 on the Baker Lake-Grandy Lake road 23 miles, to just opposite Shannon Creek Campground. Turn left on road No. 1152 for 4.5 miles. Go right on road No. (1152)014 another 1 4 miles, to where it becomes impassable, elevation 2500 feet.

Begin on an abandoned logging road overgrown with willows. At about 1 mile this road-trail enters a steep basin (see the meadows high above, keep the faith) and switchbacks twice. At 1½ miles the road ends and trail No. 742 (unsigned) begins, elevation 3200 feet. The trail climbs a steep, brush-covered clearcut made some 15 years ago and still not reforested, a heritage of the period when the College of Forestry taught that trees could be farmed to timberline.

Then, virgin forest (ain't Nature wonderful). Alternating between steep and very steep, at about 2½ miles the trail gains the ridge top and with a little down and a lot of ups leaves forest for heather meadows. The recommended turnaround is some 3 miles from the car, at the boundary of North Cascades National Park, 4700 feet. The views climax here and camping is possible on both sides of the boundary; sites on the inside have the best water and sleeping-bag spreads, but those on the outside don't require any paperwork.

A rude climbers' path leads to the pass directly above. The views there are nothing special and when snowcovered the route is slippery.

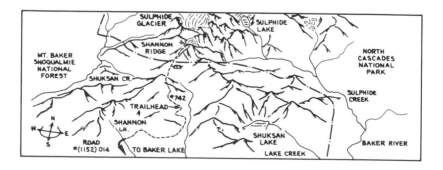

26 LITTLE SHUKSAN LAKE

Round trip 3 miles
Hiking time 5 hours
High point 4500 feet
**Elevation gain 1700 feet in, 300
feet out**

**Hikable mid-July through
September**
One day
USGS Mt. Shuksan

Be warned, this hike is strictly for agile, experienced hikers. Don't be fooled by the short 3-mile round trip. The boot-beaten path is as steep as a trail can get and not require climbing ropes and pitons. In spots it is nothing but a straight up scramble route which is becoming badly eroded and wickedly treacherous on the descent.

The hike to this small beauty spot is short, but the same can be said for climbing to the top of Seattle's Smith Tower—twice.

Drive the Baker Lake-Grandy Lake road (Hike 20) to Koma Kulshan Guard Station and 10 miles beyond. Turn left on road No. 1160, sign-described as "limited maintenance," so you won't be too surprised if there's a rockslide at about 2 miles that a passenger car may refuse to cross—or if you find other slides or slumpouts elsewhere. At a bit more than 4 switchbacking miles the road makes a final zig to climb around a cliff on a narrow roadbed blasted from solid rock; the view of Mt. Baker above is spectacular and so is that of Baker Lake, a swan dive below. At 4.7 miles the road abruptly ends in a space just big enough for a couple of cars to park and latecomers to turn around or go someplace else. Please don't block that turnaround; backing down this cliffhanger would be no picnic. The road-end is the trailhead, elevation 2800 feet.

Trail No. 608 is unmarked but obvious, starting in a huckleberry-covered clearcut. Sawn logs show that fishermen's boots have occasional help in maintenance. The path quickly enters virgin forest and climbs steeply, and more steeply, gaining 1700 feet in a scant mile up a very steep, very narrow ridge that gives a few views down to Baker River, 3000 feet below below below.

At 4500 feet the way tops the ridge and Mt. Shuksan is framed by fore-

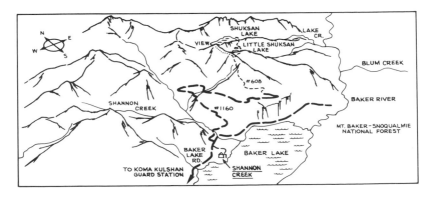

Little Shuksan Lake and Mount Blum

ground trees. The Sulphide Glacier is on the left of the summit pyramid, Crystal Glacier and Ragged Ridge on the right. For views of Mt. Baker follow the ridge ¼ mile farther to its highest point, a heather meadow.

The trail drops 300 feet to Little Shuksan Lake, 4200 feet. The fishermen's trail continues down to 3800-foot Shuksan Lake, with fish (it darn well better have something) but few views.

The "Little" is ringed by clumps of trees, fields of heather, and acres of blueberries. Though shallow, the lake has interesting bays and a picturesque island. Campsites are numerous. By midsummer the outlet dries up and the water warms up (enough for swimming).

27 BAKER RIVER

Round trip to Sulphide Creek 6
  miles
Hiking time 3–4 hours
High point 900 feet
Elevation gain 200 feet

Hikable March through
  November
One day or backpack
USGS Lake Shannon, Mt.
  Shuksan, and Mt. Challenger
Park Service backcountry use
  permit required for camping

Luxurious rain forest, a lovely milky-green river, and tantalizing glimpses of glacier-covered peaks. Because of the very low elevation (and such low-altitude virgin valleys are now rare indeed in the Cascades) the trail is open except in midwinter and offers a delightful wildland walk when higher elevations are buried in snow. Even bad weather is no barrier to enjoyment, not with all the big trees, understory plants, and streams. For a feeling of true lonesomeness, try the trip on a rainy day in early spring. It's also a good place to escape guns during hunting season, since the no-shooting North Cascades National Park is entered partway along.

Drive the Baker Lake-Grandy Lake road (Hike 20) 14 miles to Koma Kulshan Guard Station and 11.5 miles more to the lakehead. Turn left .5 mile on a spur, passing several unmarked sideroads, to the start of Upper Baker trail No. 606, elevation 760 feet.

The first ¼ mile lies on and near old logging roads, then civilization is left behind. In ½ mile is the first view—up and up the far side of the river to glaciers of 7660-foot Mt. Blum. At 1 mile the trail climbs a few feet above the river, a beautiful sight and drops again to go by large beaver ponds. In 2 miles, about where the National Park is entered, see Easy Ridge at the valley head, and a little farther on, the sharp outline of 7574-foot Whatcom Peak, northern outpost of the Pickets. In a short 3

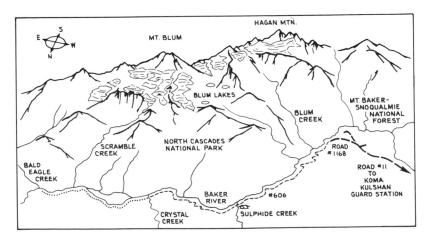

miles the way reaches raging Sulphide Creek, dominated by Jagged Ridge and its small glaciers. Partly hidden by trees is the huge expanse of the Sulphide Glacier on the south side of Mt. Shuksan.

If Sulphide Creek is high and a bridge is lacking, this is far enough for most hikers. The camp has four sites, elevation 900 feet.

Trail continues, sort of, 2 miles to Crystal Creek and once went 3 more miles to Bald Eagle Creek, 1100 feet. The upper section is now lost in brush and the best route beyond Crystal Creek is on gravel bars of the river.

Baker River

Skagit Valley from Cow Heaven; Whitehorse Mountain in distance

SKAGIT RIVER—ROSS LAKE
Unprotected area

COW HEAVEN

Round trip 11 miles
Hiking time 8 hours
High point 4400 feet
Elevation gain 4000 feet

Hikable July through October
One day
USGS Marblemount and Lake
   Shannon

Years ago, Skagit ranchers chased cows way up here to chew the alpine salads. Now only the occasional horse gobbles the flowers, so it's a heaven for hikers, with views from the Skagit Valley to the Pickets,

Eldorado, Whitehorse, and countless peaks between. But the route to heaven lies through purgatory—gaining 4000 feet in 5½ miles. Moreover, from August onward a water shortage just about forces the trip to be done in a single grueling day, though in early summer snowmelt permits camping.

Drive Highway 20 to Marblemount. At the town edge turn north .7 mile to the North Cascades National Park ranger station. Directly opposite the station take an unmarked road passing the information office. Go by a barn and small house and at 1.2 miles from the highway, where the road dead-ends at Olson Creek, spot the well-signed trailhead, elevation a meager, low-down 400 feet. The final ¼ mile of road often is washed out and must be walked. (Logging roads may change the trailhead in 1989.)

The route is signed "Cow Heaven Trail 763, 4 miles." Don't believe it—the best views are at least 5½ miles. Eager to get the job done, the path wastes no time flirting but starts steep and stays steep. The initial 2 miles are in fine shape, the tread wide and edged by soft moss, cooled by deep shadows of virgin forest. A creek is crossed at 1 mile and recrossed at 1½ miles—the last for-sure water. At about 2¼ miles the tread dips into a shallow ravine and for the next ½ mile often is gullied to naught. Just beyond 3 miles the way passes above an all-summer (usually) stream. Tall trees yield to short ones and at 4 miles to a dense tangle of mountain ash, white rhododendron, and huckleberry. At 4½ miles, about 3600 feet, a brief flat with bits of heather invites camping—but provides no lake, pond, river, creek, dribble, or spring for the purpose, only (through July?) a snowfield.

Maintained trail ends here, but a sketchy path, beaten out mainly by hunters, heads over the knoll on the skyline, climbing to the 4400-foot viewpoint. If aggrieved leg muscles and swollen tongue permit, continue up the alpine ridge to steadily broader views.

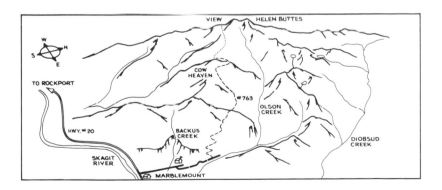

29 THORNTON LAKES— TRAPPERS PEAK

Round trip to lower Thornton
  Lake 9½ miles
Hiking time 6–8 hours
High point 4900 feet
Elevation gain 2100 feet in, 400
  feet out

Hikable mid-July through
  October
One day or backpack
USGS Marblemount
Park Service backcountry use
  permit required for camping

Three deep lakes in rock basins gouged by a long-gone glacier. Close by are living glaciers, still gouging. All around are icy peaks on the west edge of the North Cascades National Park. From a summit above the lakes, a splendid view of Triumph and Despair and the Picket Range. Not realizing they are in a national park, many hikers come here with dogs and guns and without a permit, and sometimes go away with tickets. The camping is unpleasant to miserable and not recommended unless you're there for the fishing (which also is poor). Make it a day hike.

Drive Highway 20 to Marblemount and 11 miles beyond to Thornton Creek road—spot it between mileposts 117 and 118. Turn left 5 steep miles to a parking area, elevation about 2800 feet.

The first 2 miles are on an abandoned logging road. Then begins the trail, which was never really "built" in a formal sense but just grew; it's very steep in places and mucky in others. Except for the abandoned road across clearcuts, most of the way lies in forest. At a bit more than 1 mile from the abandoned road is an opening and a small creek to jump. The trail then switchbacks up a forested slope to the ridge crest.

Recuperate atop the 4900-foot ridge crest. Look down to the lake basin and out to Mt. Triumph. Then drop 400 feet to the lowest and largest Thornton Lake. Across the outlet stream are campsites designated by posts; no fires allowed.

To reach the middle and upper lakes, traverse slopes west of the lower lake. The middle lake usually has some ice until the end of July; the upper lake, at 5000 feet in a steep-walled cirque, ordinarily is frozen until mid-August.

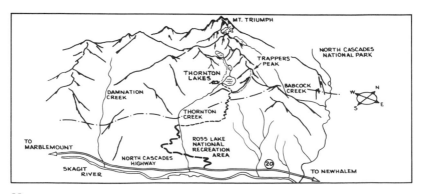

Southern Picket Range from Trappers Peak

If views are the goal, don't drop to the lakes. Leave the trail at the 4900-foot crest and follow a faint climbers' track up the ridge to the 5964-foot summit of Trappers Peak. See the fantastic Pickets. And see, too, the little village of Newhalem far below in the Skagit Valley. The route is steep in places and requires use of the hands, but is not really tough. Early in the season there may be dangerous snow patches; go above or below them. Turn around content when the way gets too scary for plain-and-simple hikers.

30 SOURDOUGH MOUNTAIN

Round trip to satellite dish 7 miles
Hiking time 7 hours
High point 4800 feet
Elevation gain 3900 feet
Hikable May through October
One day or backpack
USGS Diablo Dam and Ross Dam
Park Service backcountry use
  permit required
Round trip to summit 11 miles

Hiking time 12 hours
High point 5985 feet
Elevation gain 5100 feet
Hikable July through October

Loop trip 14 miles
Allow 2 days
High point 5985 feet
Elevation gain 4500 feet
Hikable July through October

No other hike from the Skagit River can match these views of the North Cascades National Park. Look down to Diablo Lake and Ross Lake and out to forests of Thunder Creek. Look south to the ice of Colonial and Snowfield, and southeast to Buckner and the sprawling Boston Glacier. Look east to the king of the Skagit, Jack Mountain, and north to Canada, and northwest and west to the Pickets.

There are two routes to Sourdough Mountain. One is an extremely steep trail—a strenuous day trip and not an easy weekend. The other is a loop which can be done in an arduous 2 days.

Drive Highway 20 to the Seattle City Light town of Diablo, at the base of Diablo Dam. Park in the main lot; elevation 900 feet.

Summit—Satellite dish trail: Walk back from the parking lot past the powerhouse and tennis court and find the signed trail behind the covered swimming pool. The trail starts steep and stays steep; countless short switchbacks gain 3000 feet in the first 2½ miles before the way "levels off" to an ascent of 2000 feet in the final 4 miles to the summit.

After 1½ miles of zigzags from the road up a forested hillside, an opening gives a sample of panoramas to come. At 3 miles is an unmarked junction. The left fork climbs a steep ½ mile to a satellite dish serving Diablo. For most day hikers this 4800-foot viewpoint is far enough, adding northern vistas to the southern. The way to this turnaround point often is free of snow in May, offering a spectacular springtime hike.

The main trail climbs from the junction, on a gentler grade than before, reaching a designated campsite at Sourdough Creek, 4 miles, elevation 5000 feet. (Water can be found at several places before this point, but it's thirsty travel at best.) In another 1½ miles the summit and fire-lookout cabin are attained, with all the previous views plus additional ones north up Ross Lake and west to the Pickets. Cross-country, no-fire camping is permitted on Sourdough Ridge.

Loop trail: From the parking lot, hike the unmarked ½-mile trail to the top of Diablo Dam and take the Diablo Lake passenger boat to the base of Ross Dam. Climb the road 400 feet in 1 mile to the top of Ross Dam, cross the dam, and find the Big Beaver trail. In 3 miles is a junction. Turn left on the Sourdough Mountain trail and climb 3000 feet in 4 miles to a designated campsite in Pierce Mountain saddle, and 1000 feet more in 1 mile to the 5985-foot lookout. Tread is indistinct or absent in the final rocky mile to the summit; watch for cairns. Descend to the parking lot via the "direct trail."

If two cars or a helper are available a party can shortcut the loop by driving Highway 20 eastward from Colonial Creek Campground 3.8 miles to the parking lot of the Ross Lake trailhead, elevation 1800 feet, hiking the 1 mile down to Ross Dam, and exiting to a pickup at Diablo.

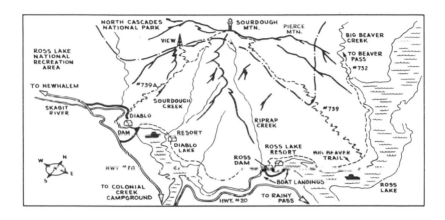

Diablo Lake from Sourdough Mountain

Pyramid Lake and Pyramid Mountain

31 PYRAMID LAKE

Round trip 4½ miles
Hiking time 3 hours
High point 2450 feet
Elevation gain 1350 feet

Hikable May through October
One day
USGS Diablo Dam and Ross Dam

Climbers pass by this tiny lake beneath the tower of 7182-foot Pyramid (actually, more cone-shaped) Peak on their way to and from ascent of Pyramid, Colonial, Paul Bunyan's Stump, and Snowfield; usually they do so before dawn and after dark, in a hurry. Fishermen don't come at all—no fish. No camping, either. So it's not exactly lonesome but there's nobody here but us family picnickers.

Drive Highway 20 east from Newhalem to the Diablo (town) junction. Keep right on the highway, crossing Gorge Lake, and .8 mile from the junction spot the Pyramid Lake trailhead, elevation 1100 feet. Park on the opposite side of the highway.

The trail climbs a short cliff and then settles into a steady ascent of very young forest (from a not-long-ago fire) with a dense understory of salal. At about ¾ mile the vegetation becomes more exciting as the way enters a narrow valley of giant old-growth trees, crosses a delightful creek, and continues uphill in a mixture of the youthful and the ancient, of the fir and the hemlock. At 2 miles note a monster of a Douglas fir leaning at such an impossible angle it surely can't last another day—as has obviously been true for many a year, if not century.

At 2¼ miles the path reaches Pyramid Lake, 2450 feet. On two sides steep cliffs plunge to the water and keep right on going down; look deep into the blue-green water and see—not the bottom—but pale faces with dull, staring eyes.

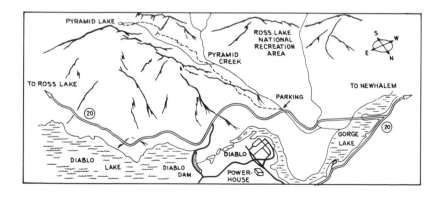

32 THUNDER CREEK

Round trip to McAllister Creek 11 miles
Hiking time 5–7 hours
High point 1800 feet
Elevation gain 600 feet
Hikable April through November
One day or backpack
USGS Ross Dam and Forbidden Peak
Park Service backcountry use permit required

Round trip to Park Creek Pass 36 miles
Allow 3–5 days
High point 6040 feet
Elevation gain 6000 feet
Hikable late July through October
USGS Ross Dam, Forbidden Peak, Mt. Logan, Goode Mountain

One of the master streams of the North Cascades, draining meltwater from an empire of glaciers. The first portion of the trail, easy walking, is nearly flat for miles, passing through groves of big firs, cedars, and hemlocks, with views of giant peaks. The route continues to a high pass amid these peaks; for experienced wilderness travelers, the trip from Thunder Creek over Park Creek Pass to the Stehekin River is a classic crossing of the range. Designated camps are scattered along the way, permitting travel by easy stages.

Drive Highway 20 to Diablo Dam and 4 miles beyond to Colonial Creek Campground, where the trail begins, elevation 1200 feet.

The trail follows Thunder Arm of Diablo Lake about 1 mile, then crosses Thunder Creek on a bridge, and in another 1 mile comes to a junction with a trail climbing to Fourth of July Pass and Panther Creek (Hike 34). The Thunder Creek trail continues straight ahead on the sidehill, going up and down a little, mainly in big trees except at 4½ miles, in a burn meadow from a lightning fire in 1971, and at 5 miles, in another from a 1970 fire; the openings give neck-stretching looks to the

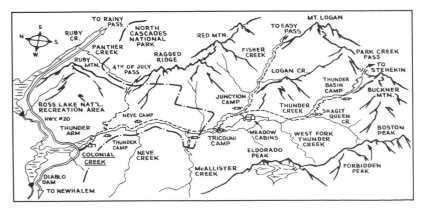

summits of Snowfield and Colonial. At about 2 and 2½ miles respectively are Thunder and Neve Camps.

At 5½ miles is the site of long-gone Middle Cabin, signed "Miners Rest Stop," and ½ mile farther is the bridge to McAllister Creek Camp, a good turnaround for a day or weekend trip. The trail to here offers one of the best forest hikes in the North Cascades and is open to travel early in the season and late.

At 6 miles the way goes from national recreation area to national park; dogs must stop. At 7½ miles the trail crosses Fisher Creek to Tricouni Camp and in ½ mile more begins a 1000-foot climb above the valley floor, which upstream from here becomes a vastness of swamp and marsh. Following Fisher Creek all the way, at 9 miles the trail levels out at Junction Camp, 3000 feet, and a junction with Fisher Creek trail (Hike 40). Off the trail a bit are grand views down to the valley and across to glaciers of Tricouni and Primus Peaks. Beyond the junction ¼ mile an obscure spur trail descends 1000 feet in 1 mile to the two Meadow Cabins, at the edge of the swamp. The main trail passes stunning viewpoints of the enormous Boston Glacier, Buckner and Boston and Forbidden thrusting above, drops steeply to the valley bottom at 2200 feet, and climbs to Skagit Queen Camp, 13 miles, 3000 feet, near where Skagit Queen Creek joins Thunder Creek. The way climbs steeply, gentles out somewhat in a hanging valley; at 15½ miles, 4300 feet, is the last designated campsite, Thunder Basin Camp. No fires. From here the trail ascends steadily up and around the meadow flanks of Mt. Logan to 6040-foot Park Creek Pass, 18 miles, a narrow rock cleft usually full of snow. To continue down to the Stehekin River, see Hike 48.

Thunder Creek trail

Big Beaver valley

SKAGIT RIVER—ROSS LAKE
North Cascades National Park

33   BEAVER LOOP

Loop trip 26½ miles
Allow 3–5 days
High point 3620 feet
Elevation gain about 3500 feet
Hikable June through October

USGS Hozomeen Mountain, Mt.
   Spickard, Mt. Challenger, Mt.
   Prophet, Pumpkin Mountain
Park Service backcountry use
   permit required for camping

This loop hike from Ross Lake to close views of the Picket Range and back to Ross Lake offers perhaps the supreme days-long forest experience in the North Cascades. The 27-mile trip up the Little Beaver valley and down the Big Beaver passes through groves of enormous cedars, old and huge Douglas firs and hemlocks, glimmery-ghostly silver fir, lush alder, young firs recently established after a fire (in 1926 enormous acreages of the Skagit country burned), and many more species and ages of trees as well. And there are brawling rivers, marshes teeming with wildlife, and awesome looks at Picket glaciers and walls.

Travel by car and trail to Ross Lake Resort (Hike 38) and arrange for taxi service up the lake and a pickup at trip's end. The loop (or day or weekend hikes) can begin at either end; the Little Beaver start is described here.

After a scenic ride up Ross Lake, debark at Little Beaver Landing; a campground here, elevation 1600 feet. The trail starts by switchbacking 800 feet to get above a canyon, then loses most of the hard-won elevation. At 4½ miles is Perry Creek Camp, an easy ford-or-footlog crossing of several branches of the creek, and a passage along the edge of a lovely marsh. At 9 miles is Redoubt Creek; scout around for a footlog. At 11½ miles, 2450 feet, is a junction.

The Little Beaver trail goes upstream 6 miles and 2800 feet to Whatcom Pass (Hike 15). Take the Big Beaver trail, which crosses Little Beaver Creek, passes a sidetrail to Stillwell Camp, and climbs a steep mile to Beaver Pass, 3620 feet. The trail goes nearly on the level a mile to designated campsites at Beaver Pass Shelter (emergency use only), the midpoint of the loop, 13½ miles from Little Beaver Landing and 13 miles from Big Beaver Landing.

An hour or three should be allowed here for an easy off trail sidetrip. Pick a way easterly and upward from the shelter, gaining 500–1000 feet through forest and brush to any of several open slopes that give a stag-

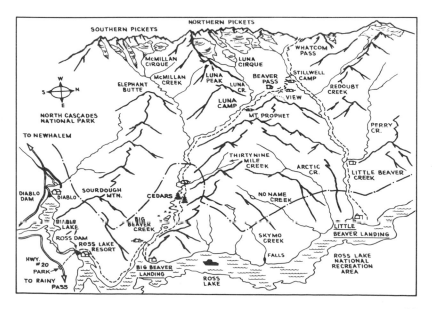

Cedar grove and Big Beaver valley trail

gering look into rough-and-icy Luna Cirque; the higher the climb the better the view.

Passing Luna Camp on the way, descend steeply from Beaver Pass into the head of Big Beaver Creek; two spots on the trail offer impressive glimpses of Luna Cirque. At 6 miles from Beaver Pass Shelter (7 miles from Big Beaver Landing on Ross Lake) the Big Beaver tumbles down a 200-foot-deep gorge; a good view here of Elephant Butte and up McMillan Creek toward McMillan Cirque. The moderately up-and-down trail crosses recent avalanches which have torn avenues through forest, passes enormous boulders fallen from cliffs above, and goes by a marsh.

At 8 miles from Beaver Pass (5½ from Ross Lake) cross Thirtynine Mile Creek; campsite. The way now enters the glorious lower reaches of Big Beaver Creek, a broad valley of marshes and ancient trees, including the largest stand of western red cedar (some an estimated 1000 years old) remaining in the United States. Seattle City Light planned to flood the lower 6 miles of the valley by raising Ross Dam, but after an epic 15-year battle, in 1983 the plans were permanently dropped.

Passing one superb marsh after another, one grove of giant cedars after another, at 3 miles from Ross Lake the trail for the first time touches the banks of Big Beaver Creek, milky-green water running over golden pebbles. Finally the trail reaches Big Beaver Landing, from which a ¼-mile trail leads left to Big Beaver Camp. (This is a boaters' camp. Hikers should use Pumpkin Mountain Camp, 100 yards south of the bridge over Big Beaver Creek on the Ross Lake trail.)

There are two ways to return to Ross Dam. One is by hiking the 6-mile Ross Lake trail, which branches right from the Big Beaver trail at a junction ¼ mile before the landing. The second is to arrange in advance with Ross Lake Resort to be picked up at Big Beaver Landing.

Canadian dogwood, or bunchberry, growing in Big Beaver valley

34 PANTHER CREEK

Round trip to Fourth of July Pass
11½ miles
Hiking time 6 hours
High point 3500 feet
Elevation gain 2300 feet

Hikable July through mid-October
One day or backpack
USGS Crater Mountain and Ross Dam
Park Service backcountry use permit required for camping

Rolling, bubbling, cascading, whirling, jumping, foaming, roaring, gurgling, singing—a whole thesaurus couldn't adequately summarize the life-style of this wondrous creek, deep in a verdant canyon between the glacial barrens of Ruby Mountain and Beebe Mountain. Follow the course for a single day of exploration or backpack to scenic camps just beyond Fourth of July Pass. If transportation can be arranged, plan a one-way trip ending at Colonial Creek Campground.

Drive Highway 20 east 8 miles from Colonial Creek Campground to Panther Creek bridge and park at the East Bank trailhead, elevation 1800 feet.

Cross the bridge to Panther Creek trail No. 758 and set out upward, switchbacking through open forest of lodgepole pine. In ¾ mile, at around 2200 feet, the trail levels off and then goes stark staring insane—turning back downvalley and losing nearly all the hardwon elevation. Giving the bemused (or embittered) hiker a final view of the Panther Creek bridge, only a whoop and a holler below, the trail comes to the creek and turns back upvalley. The ferns are lush, the red cedars ancient. Pause often to watch the creek thrashing and splashing along its narrow course. At 3 miles the way crosses the creek on a sturdy bridge to a designated campsite, a good turnaround for day hikers.

Proceeding onward, the trail soon crosses the first of several avalanche slopes and several small streams, passing from Ross Lake National Recreation Area into North Cascades National Park (Lassie, go home!).

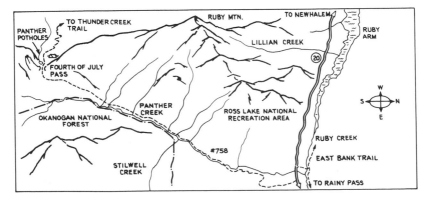

Panther Creek

At 4¾ miles, 2700 feet, the route abruptly leaves the creek and in a forest mile climbs to Fourth of July Pass, 5¾ miles, 3500 feet.

The pass is fairly flat and wide for ¼ mile, reflecting its past history as a glacier's trough. The forest is broken by small swamps. At the far end of the pass flat is an overlook of the inviting Panther Potholes. The trail then descends northward ¼ mile to Fourth of July Camp, which has a front-row seat for the big show of Colonial Peak, Neve Glacier, and Snowfield Peak.

One-way hikers are now not far from their pickup, via a quick 2½-mile drop to Thunder Creek trail and an easy 1½ miles to Colonial Creek Campground, 1240 feet, 10¼ miles from Panther Creek trailhead.

35 EAST BANK TRAIL

One-way trip from Panther Creek
to Hozomeen 31 miles
Allow 3–5 days
High point about 3500 feet
Elevation gain about 5000 feet
Hikable mid-June through
October
USGS Ross Dam, Pumpkin
Mountain, Skagit Peak,
Hozomeen Mountain
Park Service backcountry use
permit required

Round trip from Panther Creek to
Rainbow Camp 15 miles
High point 2600 feet
Elevation gain 900 feet in, 1250
feet out
Hikable May through October

When full, the reservoir known as Ross Lake simulates nature and is, indeed, a veritable inland fjord. Unfortunately, draw-downs of water for power production expose dreary wastelands of mud and stumps. Because of the low elevation, the hike along the lake is especially attractive in

Lightning Creek bridge and Ross Lake

spring, when most mountain trails are deep in snow—sorry to say, that's when the lake is at its visual worst. Generally the reservoir is full from late June to October and at a lower level other months, the maximum draw-down of as much as 150 feet usually coming in March or April. However, even when stumps are showing there still are grand views across the water to high peaks. To learn the valley in all its moods, to enjoy the panoramas from end to end, hike the East Bank Trail, mostly through forest, a little along the shore, and finally detouring inland to reach Hozomeen Campground. The complete trip can be done in several days or any portion selected for a shorter walk.

If only a portion of the trail is to be hiked, travel to Ross Dam and arrange with Ross Lake Resort for water-taxi service to the chosen beginning point and a pickup at trip's end (Hike 38).

To do the entire route drive Highway 20 the 8 miles from Colonial Creek Campground to Panther Creek Bridge and find the trailhead in the large parking area, elevation 1800 feet.

The trail drops 200 feet to the crossing of Ruby Creek and a junction beyond. Go left to Ruby Creek Barn, a scant 3 miles from the highway. The way leaves the water's edge to climb 900 feet over Hidden Hand Pass, returning to the lake near Roland Point Camp, 7½ miles.

The next 7½ miles to Lightning Creek are always near and in sight of the lake. Some stretches are blasted in cliffs; when the reservoir is full the tread is only a few feet above the waves, but when the level is down the walking is very airy. There are frequent boat-oriented camps, including the one at Lightning Creek, 16 miles from the highway.

Here the trail forks. The left continues 2 more miles up the lake, ending at the Desolation Peak trailhead (Hike 38).

For Hozomeen, take the right fork, switchback up 1000 feet to a glorious view of the lake, then lose all that elevation descending to a camp at Deer Lick Cabin (locked), 4 miles from the lake. The trail bridges Lightning Creek to a junction with the Three Fools Trail (Hike 77). Go left 7 miles to the junction with the abandoned Freezeout trail; go left on a bridge over Lightning Creek to Nightmare Camp, in a spooky cedar grove. The way leaves Lightning Creek and climbs to Willow Lake at 2853 feet, 10 miles. Another 2 miles of some ups but mostly downs lead past a sidetrail to Hozomeen Lake and at last to the road-end at Ross Lake, 31 miles from the trailhead at Panther Creek.

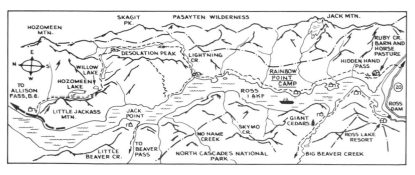

36 LITTLE JACK MOUNTAIN

Round trip to campsite 19 miles
Hiking time 9 hours
High point 6745 feet
Elevation gain 5097 feet

Hikable July through September
One day or backpack
USGS Ross Dam and Crater
  Mountain
Park Service backcountry use
  permit required for camping

Few hiker-accessible vantages in the Ross Lake area offer gazing the likes of this: up and down the fjord-like sinuosity of Ross Lake; across to Elephant Butte and up the Big Beaver valley to the heart of the Picket Range; west to Mt. Baker and Mt. Shuksan; and if that's not enough, south to such stars of the North Cascades show as Eldorado and Snowfield. So much for the good news. The trail is a bear—long, steep, and dry. Overnighters will find liquid in a small pond at Little Jack Camp but are advised not to drink it until they've used every water-purification procedure known to modern science—twice.

The trail begins at Panther Creek bridge (Hike 34), elevation 1800 feet. Descend 200 feet to Ruby Creek and a junction. Go left 2½ nearly flat miles along Ruby Creek to a major junction, 1920 feet, where the trail branches in three. Take the far right, heading back upvalley and uphill in forest toward Little Jack.

The next 6 miles have more than 60 switchbacks, all up, though not steeply. At about 4 miles views begin from the frequent openings. Progress can be measured by the dwindling size of cars streaming to and fro on Highway 20. At about 7½ miles from that thoroughfare the path enters sweetly green meadows and turns east a final mile to Little Jack Camp, 6000 feet.

The camp is separated into hiker and horse areas on either side of a scummy little pond. Come early in the summer for the snowmelt.

Just before the pond a vague sidetrail goes through a clump of trees and climbs to the ridge crest for a full panorama of Crater and Jack Mountains. The final mile of the main trail is strictly for diehards. The

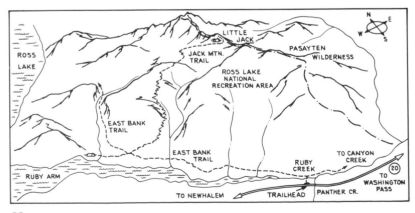

trail disappears in heather and rich blueberry meadows. Take your choice of knoll summits. The views aren't any better here than before, they just feel better. Trail tread reappears, aiming toward Jack Mountain. Forget it. Once the route leaves the meadow it's for climbers only, and not many of those because the ascent is not so much interesting as nasty, and the "King of the Skagit" is mostly allowed to reign in lonesome splendor.

Crater Mountain from shoulder of Jack Mountain

37 CRATER—DEVILS LOOP

One-way trip to Devils Dome
  Landing 27 miles; complete loop
  43 miles
Allow 5–9 days
High point 6982 feet
Elevation gain about 7500 feet
Hikable mid-July through
  October

USGS Crater Mountain, Azurite
  Peak, Shull Mountain, Jack
  Mountain, Pumpkin Mountain
Park Service backcountry use
  permit required for camping at
  Ross Lake

Hoist packs and wander meadow ridges east of Ross Lake, encircling the far-below forests of Devils Creek and the cliffs and glaciers of 8928-foot Jack Mountain, "King of the Skagit," looking to peaks and valleys from Canada to Cascade Pass, the Pickets to the Pasayten. The trip is recommended as a loop but for shorter hikes the climaxes can be reached from either end.

Drive Highway 20 eastward from Colonial Creek Campground 11 miles to Canyon Creek trailhead, elevation 1900 feet.

The way begins by crossing Granite Creek on a substantial bridge, going downsteam a bit and crossing Canyon Creek on a commodious footlog.

Once across Canyon Creek the work begins—the trail gains 3400 feet in 4 miles. Fortunately, the labor is mostly shaded by big trees and there is water at several well-spaced points and ultimately glimpses of peaks. At 4 miles, 5280 feet, is a junction.

For a compulsory sidetrip, go left ¾ mile to the impressive cirque and shallow waters of 5800-foot Crater Lake. Just before the meadow-and-cliff-surrounded lake, a 2-mile trail climbs eastward to a lookout site on the broad, 7054-foot easternmost summit of Crater Mountain. From the lake a 2½-mile trail climbs westward to another lookout site on the 8128-foot main summit of Crater; the final ½ mile is for trained climbers only, but the panoramas are glorious long before difficulties begin. When this higher lookout was manned, the final cliff was scaled with the help of wooden ladders and fixed ropes. Maintenance proved too difficult and summit clouds too persistent causing installation of the lower lookout. Now both cabins are long gone.

From the 4-mile junction the trail descends the gently sloping table of McMillan Park to Nickol Creek, 4900 feet, then climbs an old burn, loaded with blueberries in season, to Devils Park Shelter, 7 miles, 5600 feet. (This and the other shelters are not maintained but will be left as they are until too dangerous, then demolished.) One can roam for hours in this plateau of meadows, clumps of alpine trees, and bleached snags.

The way now climbs northward along Jackita Ridge into a larch-dotted basin. At 8¾ miles, some 6200 feet, is a junction of sorts. The well-maintained Jackita Ridge trail No. 753, the main route, continues up

Crater Mountain

across the basin. The long-abandoned alternate, Hells Basin trail, un-signed and with no tread at first, climbs to the 6700-foot ridge crest, drops more than 1000 feet into stark Hells Basin, regains the elevation to climb over Anacortes Crossing, and loses it again to rejoin the Jackita Ridge trail.

From the unmarked junction at 8¾ miles the main route ascends a shoulder, switchbacks 800 feet down a slate scree to a rocky basin, rounds another shoulder and drops 300 feet into another open basin, climbs 500 feet to a third shoulder, drops 1000 feet through meadows and forest to North Fork Devils Creek, and ascends very steeply upstream ½ mile to the 5500-foot junction with the trail to Anacortes Crossing— which is some 1500 feet and 1 mile from here, and another compulsory sidetrip. Main-route distance to this junction, 13¼ miles.

The trail traverses sweeping gardens of Jackita Ridge, up some and down more, to Devils Pass, 15¼ miles, 5800 feet. The best camping is at Devils Pass Shelter, several hundred feet and ½ mile below the pass in a pretty meadow with a year-round spring, reached via the Deception Pass trail and then a sidetrail.

From Devils Pass the way turns west on the Devils Ridge trail, going through open woods near and on the ridge top, then climbing a lush basin to Skyline Camp, 18 miles, 6300 feet—a lovely spot for a star-bright sleep but with no water after the snows are gone. (In fact, there is no de-pendable water between North Fork Devils Creek and Dry Creek Pass.)

A flower-and-blueberry traverse and a short ridge-crest ascent lead, at 20 miles, to the 6982-foot site of the demolished Devils Dome Lookout, the highest elevation of the main-route trail.

Now down into a basin of waterfalls and boulders and blossoms and around the flowery slopes of Devils Dome, with time out for a com-pulsory, easy-walking, off-trail roaming to the 7400-foot summit and

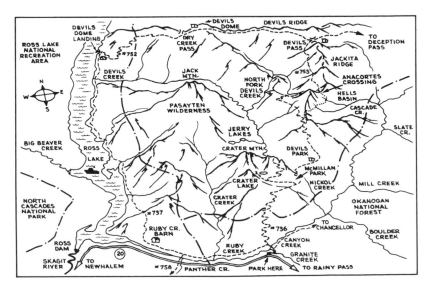

wide horizons. At 21½ miles is a ¼-mile sidetrail to 6000-foot Bear Skull Shelter, the first possible camp if the loop is being done in the reverse direction and a long day—5½ miles and 4500 feet—above Ross Lake.

At last the highlands must be left. The trail goes down the crest a short bit to Dry Creek Pass, descends forests and burn meadows to the only dependable creek, at 23 miles, enters young trees (hot and grueling to climb in sunny weather) of an old burn, crosses the East Bank Trail, and ¼ mile later, at 27 miles, ends at the lakeside camp of Devils Dome Landing.

To return to the start, either hike the East Bank Trail (Hike 35) or, by prearranged pickup, ride back in a boat of Ross Lake Resort (Hike 38).

Crater Lake

38 DESOLATION PEAK

Round trip from Desolation
Landing 9 miles
Hiking time 7 hours
High point 6085 feet
Elevation gain 4400 feet

Hikable mid-June through
August
One day (from the lake) or
backpack
USGS Hozomeen Mountain
Park Service backcountry use
permit required for camping

A forest fire swept the slopes bare in 1926, giving the peak its name. The lookout cabin on the summit gained fame in literary circles after being manned for a summer by the late Jack Kerouac, "beat generation" novelist and sometime Forest Service employee. Some of his best writing describes the day-and-night, sunshine-and-storm panorama from the Methow to Mt. Baker to Canada, and especially the dramatic close-up of Hozomeen Mountain, often seen from a distance but rarely from so near. Before and since Kerouac, the lookout frequently has been manned by poets. The steep trail is a scorcher in sunny weather; carry lots of water.

The start of the Desolation Peak trail can be reached by walking 18 miles on the East Bank Trail (Hike 35) or by riding the water taxi. For the latter, drive Highway 20 eastward from Colonial Creek Campground 3.8 miles to the parking lot of the Ross Dam trailhead, elevation 1800 feet. But before this, from home or while driving up the Skagit Valley, telephone Ross Lake Resort. (There is no direct telephone service to the resort, but contact can be made. Dial "Operator," ask for "Everett Operator," give the number 397-7735, and make arrangements. Bring cash— the taxi man will not accept checks or credit cards.) Then, from the trailhead, drop 200 feet to the dam and boat dock opposite the resort; here the resort boat will ferry you to your destination and return to pick you up at a prearranged time.

The trail starts steep and stays steep, climbing 1000 feet a mile. For such a desolate-appearing hillside there is a surprising amount of shade, the way often tunneling through dense thickets of young trees. This is

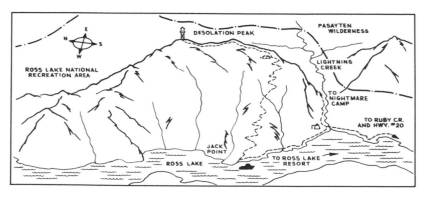

Jack Mountain on left and Ross Lake from Desolation Peak

fortunate because the sun can be unmerciful on the occasional barren bluffs.

Views come with every rocky knoll. In ½ mile see a small grove of birch trees. In 2 miles there is a spring—which may, however, dry up in a rainless summer. At 3 miles the trail enters steep, open meadows and at 4 miles is the ridge crest. A high bump remains to be climbed over before the lookout is sighted. The flower fields include some species that properly "belong" on the east slopes of the Cascades.

The horizons are broad and rich. Only Mt. Baker stands out distinctly among the distant peaks, though those who know them can single out Shuksan, the Pickets, Colonial, Snowfield, Eldorado, and scores of other great mountains. Closer in, the spectacular glacier of 8928-foot Jack Mountain dominates the south. To the north rise the vertical walls of Hozomeen. West across Ross Lake are the deep valleys of No Name Creek, Arctic Creek, and Little Beaver Creek. East are the high, meadow-roaming ridges of the Cascade Crest and the Pasayten country.

The fjordlike Ross Lake reservoir, dotted by tiny boats of fishermen, is the feature of the scene. Unfortunately, from fall to spring miles of dreary mudflats are exposed as the reservoir is drawn down; plan the trip for summer when the full reservoir adorns rather than desecrates the Ross Lake National Recreation Area.

There is a designated campsite (no fires) in the trees just below the high meadows; water is from snowfields only and usually rare or nonexistent by late July. Because of the time spent getting to the trailhead, the best plan for a weekend trip is to travel the first day to Lightning Creek Camp, stay there overnight, and do the climb the second day.

39 CANYON CREEK

Round trip to Miners Creek 14 miles
Hiking time 8 hours
High point 2600 feet
Elevation gain 700 feet
Hikable June through October
One day or backpack
USGS Azurite Peak and Crater Mountain

Round trip to Boulder Creek 7 miles
Hiking time 4 hours
High point 2400 feet
Elevation gain 500 feet

Walk a canyon-narrow valley through groves of giant trees, past waterfalls, and then on what obviously is the remnant of an ancient road, though one who didn't know there was such a thing as a specially-made narrow-gauge truck would marvel what sort of vehicle ever traveled it. (No mystery nowadays—the Forest Service has handed the historical artifact over to the mercies of the vroom-vroomers.) Once a main route

Pyrola

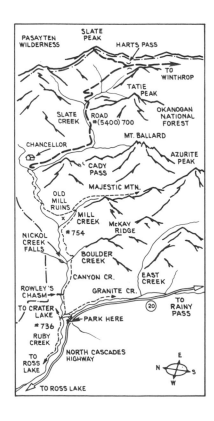

A peek at Snowfield Peak from Canyon Creek trail

from the Skagit Valley to gold fields of the Harts Pass area (the mother lode was—and still is—located in distant cities, worked by stock salesmen), lined by an almost continuous string of mining claims, many with cabins, the trail eventually reaches Chancellor, a thriving community in 1880, now a ghost town at the end of the road down from Harts Pass. If transportation can be arranged (and if the trail is known in advance to be passable the whole way), start at Chancellor and hike downstream. Otherwise, start at the lower end and hike upstream. The 3½ miles to Boulder Creek are a fine day hike. If backpacking, continue to Mill Creek, 7 miles, for campsites. But if the trail has slid out at the several spots where it is wont to do so, turn back.

For the lower start, drive Highway 20 to Canyon Creek trail No. 754 (Hike 37). From the east side of the parking lot follow Granite Creek upstream 100 feet to a bridge. Cross to a trail junction and take the right.

The big trees and the creek provide entertainment. So does keeping an eye out for collapsed cabins and rusty tools, though the generations of wet rot and green jungling have left precious little evidence of the mining (prospecting, stock-selling) excitement. Conjure up a vision of Owen Wister and his bride riding down the trail on their honeymoon journey from the Methow Valley to Western Washington.

In a scant 2 miles take a short sidetrip to Rowley's Chasm, where the narrow walls almost touch; the chasm is spanned by a bridge scarcely 10 feet long, a giddy 100 feet and then some above the water. Proceeding onward, look through trees to a good view of Crater Mountain, and at 3 miles to the white splash of Nickol Creek Falls. At 3½ miles, 2400 feet, Boulder Creek may have to be forded, which at high water may be too neat a trick.

At 7 miles, 2600 feet, trail ends and narrow-gauge road (and motorcycles) begin at Mill Creek. Campers will want to poke about such scant remains as may be found of the sawmill built to supply mine timbers.

At 9 miles from Highway 20, at 3000 feet, is Chancellor and the end of the road from Harts Pass (Hike 74).

40 EASY PASS—FISHER CREEK

Round trip to Easy Pass 7 miles
Hiking time 7 hours
High point 6500 feet
Elevation gain 2800 feet
Hikable mid-July through
  September
One day or backpack
USGS Mt. Arriva and Mt. Logan
Park Service backcountry use
  permit required for camping

One-way trip from Easy Pass to
  Colonial Creek Campground 19
  miles
Allow 3–4 days
Elevation gain 5300 feet

Dramatic are the views, but the trail definitely is not easy. Prospectors found this the easiest (maybe the only) pass across Ragged Ridge, and thus the name. However, the tread is rough, at times very steep, and in spots muddy. Finally, the pass area is very small, extremely fragile, and camping is not allowed.

Drive Highway 20 east 21.5 miles from Colonial Creek Campground or 6.2 miles west from Rainy Pass to an unmarked spur road and parking area, elevation 3700 feet.

In a short ¼ mile the trail crosses Granite Creek on a footlog and then climbs 2 miles in woods to the edge of a huge avalanche fan, 5200 feet, under the rugged peaks of Ragged Ridge. The trail now may become elusive, buried in snow or greenery. (Make very sure not to lose the path; cross-country exploration here is agonizing.) The way goes over the avalanche fan and Easy Pass Creek and begins a long, steep ascent along the south side of the valley to the pass. Flower gardens. Small groves of

Western anemone

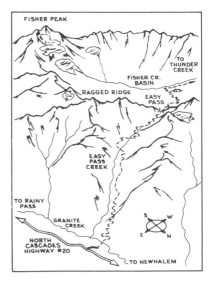

Fisher Creek valley and Mount Logan

trees. Watercourses. Boulder fields. Up, always up. The route crosses
Easy Pass Creek twice more and at about 6100 feet comes within a few
feet of a gushing spring, the source of the creek. Tread shoveled from a
steep talus slope leads to the 6500-foot pass, a narrow, larch-covered
saddle.

For the best views wander meadows up the ridge above the pass and
look down 1300 feet into Fisher Creek Basin and out to glaciers and
walls of 9080-foot Mt. Logan.

To continue to Diablo Lake, descend 1½ miles to a designated no-fire
camp in Fisher Basin, 5200 feet. At 5½ miles is Cosho Camp and, just
beyond, a footlog crossing of Fisher Creek. At 10½ miles is Junction
Camp, where is met the Thunder Creek trail (Hike 32), which leads to
Colonial Creek Campground at 19 miles from the pass.

Lookout Mountain and Eldorado Peak

CASCADE RIVER
Partly in North Cascades National Park

LOOKOUT MOUNTAIN— MONOGRAM LAKE

**Round trip to Lookout Mountain
8½ miles
Hiking time 9 hours
High point 5719 feet
Elevation gain 4500 feet
Hikable mid-July through
October
One day or backpack
USGS Marblemount**

**Round trip to Monogram Lake 7½
miles
Hiking time 9 hours
High point 5400 feet
Elevation gain 4200 feet in, 600
feet out
Park Service backcountry use
permit required for camping**

Take your pick: a fire lookout (maintained now by volunteers) with a commanding view of North Cascades peaks and valleys, or a cirque lake, a fine basecamp for roaming, nestled in the side of a heather-covered ridge.

Drive Highway 20 to Marblemount and continue east 7 miles on the Cascade River road to the 1200-foot trailhead between Lookout and Monogram Creeks.

The trail climbs steeply in a series of short switchbacks along the spine of the forested ridge between the two creeks, gaining 2400 feet in the 2½ miles to a campsite at the first dependable water, a branch of Lookout Creek at 3600 feet. At 2¾ miles is a junction, elevation 4200 feet.

Lookout Mountain: Go left from the junction, shortly emerging into meadow and switchbacking relentlessly upward. The tread here may be hard to find and difficult to walk. In 1½ miles from the junction, gaining 1500 feet, the 5719-foot summit is attained.

Flowers all around—and views. Look north and west to the Skagit River Valley, southeast and below to the Cascade River. Mountains everywhere, dominated by giant Eldorado Peak. About ¼ mile below the summit, in a small flat, is a spring that runs most of the summer. Magnificent camps here for enjoyment of the scenery in sunset and dawn—but disaster camps in a storm.

Monogram Lake: Traverse right from the junction on a steep, lightly timbered hillside. The trail leaves trees for meadow and in a mile crosses a creek, climbs to a 5400 foot crest with broad views, and descends to 4800-foot Monogram Lake, usually snowbound through July. Designated no-fire campsites around the meadow shores.

The lake is a superb base for wanderings. For one, climb open slopes to the southeast and then follow the ridge northerly to a 5607-foot knoll looking down into Marble Creek and across to the splendor of 8868-foot Eldorado—a closer and even better view of the peak than that from Lookout Mountain. Continue on the ridge for more flowers, then drop through gardens to the lake. For a more ambitious tour, ascend meadows on the southern extension of Teebone Ridge and ramble to the 6844-foot south summit of Little Devil Peak, with looks down to small glaciers. Climbers can continue on and on along the rocky-and-snowy ridge, but hikers must stop when the terrain gets too rough for party experience.

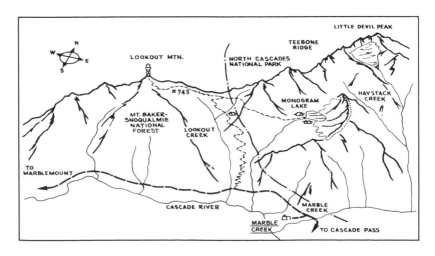

42 HIDDEN LAKE PEAKS

Round trip to Sibley Creek Pass 6 miles
Hiking time 5 hours
High point 6100 feet
Elevation gain 2700 feet
Hikable mid-July through October
One day or backpack
USGS Eldorado Peak and Sonny Boy Lakes
Park Service backcountry use permit required for camping at Hidden Lake

Round trip to Hidden Lake Lookout 8 miles
Hiking time 8 hours
High point 6890 feet
Elevation gain 3500 feet
Hikable August through October

Flower fields, heather meadows, ice-carved rocks, and snow-fed waterfalls on an alpine ridge jutting into an angle of the Cascade River valley, providing an easy-to-reach viewpoint of the wilderness North Cascades from Eldorado through the Ptarmigan Traverse to Dome Peak.

Drive Highway 20 to Marblemount and continue east on the Cascade River road 9.5 miles (2 miles past the Marble Creek bridge) to Sibley Creek road No. 1540. Turn left 4.7 miles to road-end (the way rough but passable to suitably small and spry cars) in a clearcut, elevation 3400 feet.

Trail No. 745 begins in the brush that 30 years after the logging still doesn't look much like a "renewable resource," entering virgin forest in ¼ mile and switchbacking upward 1 mile. The way then emerges from trees into lush brush and crosses Sibley Creek. (Some years avalanche snow may linger in the creek bottom all summer, in which case look for obvious trail cut through very steep sidehill greenery.) The trail switchbacks up alder clumps and deep grass and flowers to a recrossing of Sibley Creek at 2½ miles, 5200 feet. Note, here, the abrupt transition from metamorphic to granitic rocks, the first supporting richly green

Clark's nutcracker

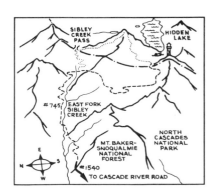

Hidden Lake and Sahale Peak, center

herbaceous flora, the other dominated by heather. Just past the crossing is a minimal campsite.

Hidden Lake Lookout: From the second crossing the trail traverses wide-open heather-and-waterfall slopes (several nice good-weather camps), then rounds a corner and climbs. One snow-filled gully may be too treacherous for hikers lacking ice axes. If so, don't attempt to cross, but instead go straight uphill to find a safe detour, or turn back and visit Sibley Creek Pass. The trail may be snow-covered at other points but by proceeding straight ahead the tread can be picked up. At 3½ miles is a tiny basin, a lovely nonstorm campsite. The abandoned lookout cabin can now be seen atop cliffs. Continue a short way, usually on a gentle snow-field, to the 6600-foot saddle and look down to Hidden Lake and out to a world of wild peaks.

Though it's only ½ mile and 300 feet from the saddle to the broader views of the 6890-foot lookout (maintained by volunteers), parts of the trail may be lost in extremely dangerous snow, suited only for trained climbers. Even without snow the final section of trail is airy.

From the saddle an easy walk over loose boulders leads to the 7088-foot highest summit of Hidden Lake Peaks. Or descend rough talus to the 5733-foot lake, ordinarily snowbound through most of the summer. Designated no-fire campsites above the lake.

43 BOSTON BASIN

**Round trip to first high moraine 7
  miles**
Hiking time 8 hours
High point 6200 feet
Elevation gain 3000 feet
Hikable July through October

One day or backpack
**USGS Cascade Pass and
  Forbidden Peak**
**Park Service backcountry use
  permit required for camping**

After Forbidden Peak was included in a book as one of the "50 classic
climbs in North America," the meadowlands of Boston Basin began to be
infested by climbers from all over North America seeking the 50 Peak
Pin. Since a normal hiker—finding himself amid a throng of 60 or 70
peakbaggers clicking carabiners—is liable to start screaming, and since
the trail is unmaintained and poor, and since the camping is lousy, why
go? Well, on a Tuesday or Thursday in late October, when the classicists
are back in school, a person might just sneak up to the basin for a day
and find the solitude proper for savoring the contrast of yellowing meadows and gray moraines and white glaciers.

Drive Highway 20 to Marblemount and continue east on the Cascade
River road 23.5 miles to the Diamond Mine junction. Park here, elevation 3200 feet.

Begin by walking 1 steep mile on abandoned road to the Diamond
Mine, which didn't dig for diamonds or much of anything else except the

Mount Johannesburg from Boston Basin

cash that could be extracted from investors and ultimately settled for a rich strike in the coffers of the National Park Service. Continue upward on a climbers' scramble-path that intersects an ancient miners' trail. Miners of old did neater work than modern climbers, so things improve. Vintage tread leads through a short bit of woods and then across a ½-mile-wide swath of avalanche greenery, down which roar Midas Creek and Morning Star Creek. Next come switchbacks in deep forest to a broken-down mine cabin.

About ¼ mile from the wrecked cabin the trail emerges from timber and swings around the foot of an open moraine to a raging torrent; boulder-hop across (the best crossing is upstream from where the trail meets the creek) and climb to a viewpoint atop the moraine. Look up to the fearsome cliffs and spires of Forbidden Peak and Mt. Torment, and to the glacier falling from Boston and Sahale Peaks, and across the valley to the mile-high wall of Johannesburg and its fingerlike hanging glaciers.

For one exploration of Boston Basin, traverse and climb westward over moraines and creeks to rich-green, marmot-whistling flower fields and beyond the waterfalls pouring down ice-polished buttresses under Mt. Torment.

For another exploration, look for intermittent tread of an old miners' trail that ascends a moraine crest to tunnels and artifacts close under Sharkfin Tower, right next to the glacier falling from Boston Peak.

A spectacular for the experienced highland rambler only: Climb moraines and meadows to Sahale Arm and descend to Cascade Pass; those capable of doing the tour need no further clues.

To conclude, there's a world of wandering in Boston Basin, if you can get there when the place isn't up to the scuppers in ropes and hard hats. However, absolutely no camping is allowed in the meadows. You must stay at the 5800-foot "climbers' camp," three sites, bouldery and wretched, just above timberline between the forks of Boston Creek, or up high on the snow or rock; if in doubt, go with the latter.

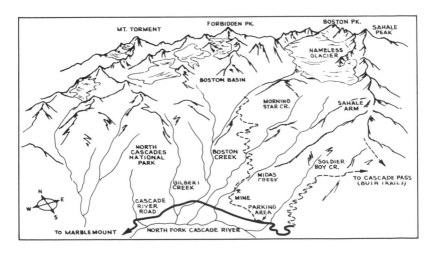

44 CASCADE PASS—SAHALE ARM

Round trip to Cascade Pass 7 miles	**Round trip to Sahale Arm 11 miles**
Hiking time 5 hours	**Hiking time 10 hours**
High point 5400 feet	**High point 7600 feet**
Elevation gain 1800 feet	**Elevation gain 4000 feet**
Hikable mid-July through October	**Hikable mid-July through October**
One day	**One day or backpack**
USGS Cascade Pass	**Park Service backcountry use permit required**

An historic pass, crossed by Indians from time immemorial, by explorers and prospectors since early in the 19th century, and recently become famous as one of the most rewarding easy hikes in the North Cascades. But the beauty of the pass is only the beginning. An idyllic ridge climbs toward the sky amid flowers and creeklets of sparkling water and views that expand with every step.

Drive Highway 20 to Marblemount and continue east 25 miles on the Cascade River road to road-end parking lot and trailhead, 3600 feet.

In some 33 switchbacks the 10-percent grade "highway" climbs forest about 2 miles, then makes a long, gently ascending traverse through parkland and meadows to Cascade Pass, 3½ miles, 5400 feet. Spectacular as the scenery is from road-end, the hiker runs out of superlatives before reaching the pass. The 8200-foot mass of Johannesburg dominates: Hardly an hour goes by that a large or small avalanche doesn't break loose from its hanging glacier; several times a summer a huge section of ice roars all the way to the valley floor.

Cascade Pass retains its famous vistas, but during years of overuse the meadows were loved nearly to death. The Park Service is seeking to rehabilitate the flower gardens and thus camping and fires are forbidden at the pass. However, a few campsites are available below the pass to the east, in Pelton Basin, enabling a longer stay for extended sidetrips.

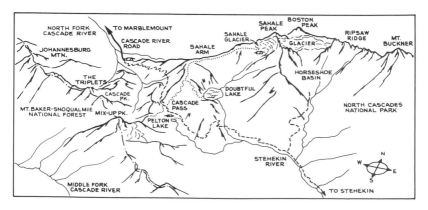

(There also are several cozy pack-in sites close by the road-end—as scenic camps as one could want.)

One sidetrip from the pass, easy and quick, is the wandering way south up the meadow crest of Mixup Arm.

To explore the sky, climb north on a steep and narrow trail through meadows; find the start a few feet over the east side of the pass below a rock outcrop. In 1 mile and 800 feet the trail reaches the ridge crest and a junction. The right fork descends heather 800 feet in 1 mile to 5385-foot Doubtful Lake, a great hike in its own right, the shore cliffs riddled with old mines.

However, Sahale Arm calls. Walk the old prospectors' trail up and along the gentle ridge of flowers, and up some more. Look down to the waterfall-loud cirque of Doubtful Lake and east into the Stehekin River valley. Look west to Forbidden Peak and the huge Inspiration Glacier on Eldorado. Look south to nine small glaciers on the first line of peaks beyond Cascade Pass. Walking higher, see range upon range of ice and spires, finally including the volcano of Glacier Peak. To see it all in sunset and starlight and dawn, camp in the rocks at the toe of the Sahale Glacier—this is permitted. No fires. (No wood.)

Magic Mountain and cloud-filled Cascade Pass from Sahale Arm

45 CHELAN LAKESHORE TRAIL

One-way trip from Prince Creek
17½ miles
Allow 3–4 days
High point 1700 feet
Elevation gain perhaps 3000 feet
Hikable late March through early
June

USGS Lucerne, Prince Creek, Sun
Mountain, Stehekin

One-way trip from Moore 6½
miles
Allow 2 days
High point 1600 feet
Elevation gain about 900 feet

The way to know Lake Chelan is to walk beside it, sometimes by waves slapping the shore, sometimes on high bluffs with sweeping views. There are green lawns atop rock buttresses, groves of old Ponderosa pine and Douglas fir, glades of mystic aspen, slot gorges with frothing waterfalls. The views and trees and many of the creeks are grand in any season but spring is the prime time, when the sun is dependable but not too weighty, cool breezes blow, and the flowers are in rich bloom. Early on, the trail is lined by trillium, chocolate lily, glacier lily, spring beauty, yellowbells, Johnny-jump-up, red currant, and more. Later on, the show features spring gold, prairie star, blue-eyed Mary, naked broomrape, primrose monkeyflower, death camas, balsamroot, miners lettuce, calypso, and more.

Note: By early summer the country gets so dry that wood fires within 1 mile of the shore are banned except where metal rings are provided— namely, at Prince Creek, Moore, and Fish Creek Shelter. Carry a stove. You should've come earlier anyhow.

Drive to the town of Chelan or up the lake to Field Point and board the passenger boat *Lady of the Lake.* Contact the National Park Service— Forest Service Information Center in Seattle to learn the current sched-

Lake Chelan and McGregor Mountain from Hunts Bluff

ule. The past pattern has been a single trip daily from mid-May to mid-September, uplake in early morning, downlake in early afternoon, and Sunday-Monday-Wednesday-Friday trips the rest of the year (no Sunday boat in midwinter).

For a 2-day trip, hikers can start at Moore with day packs and have their overnight gear dumped on the dock at Stehekin to await them; this gives an afternoon on the trail and a morning poking around Stehekin.

To do the full 17½ miles from Prince Creek to Stehekin the nice allowance is 4 days (including the going-home day) though 3 are tolerable.

The map fails to say that though the trail never climbs higher than 1700 feet and generally is some several hundred feet above the shore (1098 feet above sea level), it irrationally manages to go uphill virtually the whole way.

At Prince Creek hikers have the choice of being put off downlake from the creek, perhaps to stay the first night at the campground there, or uplake (a campsite here, too) to save ½ mile of trail.

Since the debarkation at Prince Creek is about 11 a.m., most hikers camp the first night in the vicinity of Meadow Creek, 7 miles, after crossing Rattlesnake, Rex, Pioneer, and Cascade Creeks. The shelter cabin in the dark woods at Meadow Creek is unattractive except in a storm.

By the nice plan, a relaxed second day attains the trail's high point at 1700 feet on a long, wide shelf, descends to Fish Creek, 10½ miles from Prince Creek, then takes the sidetrail ½ mile down the creek to Moore's Point, once a famous resort and now a spacious Forest Service campground. Spend the afternoon exploring the ancient orchard and the New Englandlike stone walls fencing a deer pasture.

The 6½ miles from Fish Creek to Stehekin are an easy morning for a 3-day trip. (Since the boat doesn't go downlake until afternoon, a party can finish the trip the morning of "boat day.") The way starts by climbing to 1600 feet on Hunts Bluff and its climactic views of lake and mountains. The trail then drops to the lake, crossing more creeks, and comes to Lakeshore (Flick Creek) Shelter, a choice camp on a jut of forest and rock out into the waves. It never again climbs high, wandering the base of cliffs and through woods to Flick Creek, Fourmile Creek, Hazard Creek, and finally Stehekin, 17½ miles. (To be technical, the sign here says "Fish Creek 6.6, Prince Creek 17.2.")

Overnight camping is permitted where the trail enters the Stehekin complex (this campground is designated "overflow") and ¼ mile up the road at Purple Point Campground.

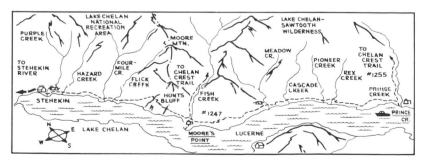

46   RAINBOW LOOP

Loop trip 6 miles (using
  shuttlebus) or 9 miles (without)
Hiking time 5 hours (or 7 hours)
High point 2600 feet
Elevation gain 1500 feet

Hikable March through
  November
One day or backpack
USGS Stehekin
Park Service backcountry use
  permit required for camping

The high country of Stehekin is a long way up and for much of the year is up to a hiker's eyebrows in snow. The low country, on the other hand, offers relaxed walking almost year-round.

A favorite plan, especially among families with small children, is to take the boat to Stehekin (Hike 45), then the Park Service shuttlebus 5 miles up the Stehekin Road, and establish camp on the banks of the Stehekin River at Harlequin (formerly Company Creek) Campground, elevation 1195 feet. By walking the short bit out from the campground and across the Harlequin Bridge, a party can be whisked by shuttlebus up the Stehekin Road to any number of trailheads that provide nice day hikes: Agnes Gorge, Coon Lake, Flat Creek, Park Creek, and others. The party then can be whisked back to Harlequin for supper.

Contact the National Park Service Information Center in Seattle before the trip to learn the current bus schedule. The past pattern has been several round trips daily from spring to fall.

The bus isn't needed for the Stehekin River Trail, which takes off from the campground and in 4 flat and easy downstream miles of forest flowers and river vistas emerges at Weaver Point Campground, on the shore of Lake Chelan; the swimming is invigorating.

The bus also isn't needed, though it can be used, for the classic Rainbow Loop. The upper and lower trailheads are a scant 3 miles apart on the Stehekin Road; the walk between them can be enlivened by a cooling sidetrip to Rainbow Falls and a tour of the historic Stehekin School.

Note: Rainbow has a reputation as the snakiest trail in the valley, but on none of his trips has the surveyor ever seen a rattler. However, standard precautions are in order while admiring the penstemon, cinquefoil,

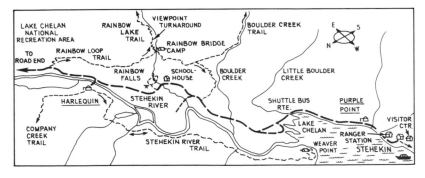

death camas, monkeyflower, naked broomrape, linear phacelia, salmon collomia, willow herb, broadleaf montia, balsamroot, lupine, stonecrop, lava alumroot, paintbrush, tiger lily, larkspur, suksdorfia, buckwheat, sandwort, luina, arnica, pinedrops, prairie star, snowbrush, and friends.

The recommended start is the upper trailhead, elevation 1240 feet, a long ½ mile up the valley road from Harlequin Bridge. Views through the forest grow steadily on the 2½-mile ascent to a junction, 2150 feet. The views here are very big, but don't be satisfied.

Sidetrip up the left fork, the Rainbow Lake trail, a long ½ mile to where it zigs right at 2600 feet. Zag left, out onto a bald slope of rock slabs and green grass. Find a piece of soft granite to sit on, break out the pickle sandwiches and the jug of orange juice, and gaze: Across the valley to massive Si Si Ridge, crags of Devore Peak, the tower of Tupshin; but especially, out to Lake Chelan, rippled by wind, sparkling in sun, and down the long fjord to Moore's Point, Domke Mountain, and the big peaks of Milham Pass.

Having returned from the sidetrip to the junction, descend 2½ miles to the lower trailhead, passing on the way: A few feet from the junction, Rainbow Creek, with a nice little woods camp; the Boulder Creek trail, branching left; a series of switchbacks on the naked valley wall, with more views of the lake and others straight down to the river, one meander picturesquely enwrapping Buckner's Orchard; Boulder Creek. The road is reached at 1160 feet, 2½ miles from Stehekin Landing.

If the trip schedule is meshed with the bus schedule, a party can ride back to Harlequin. However, it's only 2¼ miles up the road. Halfway along are the Stehekin School and the short sideroad and path to Rainbow Falls, where sunburnt hikers have been known to sit in forest shadows and let the billows of spray wash over them until their pink skin turns a nice shade of blue.

Lake Chelan from Rainbow Lake trail (Harvey Manning photo)

47 NORTH FORK BRIDGE CREEK

Round trip to cirque 21 miles
Allow 2–3 days
High point 4200 feet
Elevation gain 2000 feet

Hikable early July through
October
USGS McGregor Mountain and
Mt. Logan
Park Service backcountry use
permit required for camping

The North Cascades are distinguished by tall peaks—and also by deep holes. Among the most magnificent holes in the range is the huge cirque at the head of North Fork Bridge Creek, where breezes ripple meadow grasses beneath the ice-hung precipices of 9160-foot Goode Mountain, 8515-foot Storm King Peak, and 9087-foot Mt. Logan.

Travel to Bridge Creek, 16 miles from Stehekin (Hikes 45 and 46). Just before the creek is the trailhead, elevation 2200 feet. The trail starts with a short, stiff climb of 400 feet, then goes up and down in woods, emerging to a view of Memaloose Ridge and reaching the bridge over Bridge Creek at 2½ miles, 2600 feet. Across the bridge and ¼ mile beyond is a junction; go left on the North Fork trail.

The way ascends steeply a bit and gentles out. From brushy openings in the forest are views of rugged cliffs—a promise of what is to come. To achieve fulfillment of the promise it is necessary to camp somewhere in the North Fork. There are three choices: Walker Park Camp, 5½ miles, 3120 feet, a miserable, fly-ridden pit; Grizzly Creek Camp, about 6 miles, 3200 feet, in open woods near the stream; and Grizzly Creek Horse Camp, 6⅓ miles, 3180 feet.

The ford of Grizzly Creek is not life-threatening except in snowmelt season, yet neither are its wide, cold, rushing waters a novice's joy. Beyond the creek the way leaves woods and wanders along the valley bottom in cottonwood groves, avalanche brush, and patches of grass. Immense views continue—up and up the 6000-foot north wall of Goode to icefalls of the Goode Glacier and towers of the summit.

At 7¼ miles, about 1⅔ miles past Grizzly Creek, maintained trail ends in North Fork Meadows. The old path continues, a bit less gentle. At about 9½ miles, 3800 feet, is the site of famous Many Waterfalls Camp,

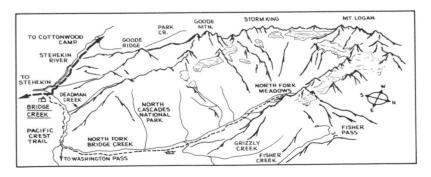

Mount Goode and North Fork Bridge Creek (Dick Brooks photo)

where camping is now banned. The scene is glorious with wide fields of hip-high grass, the roar of many waterfalls from hanging glaciers, and neck-stretching gazes to Goode and Storm King.

Paths here are confusing; climb the brushy knoll above to a resumption of tread amid small and sparse trees. In a stand of old alpine timber that has escaped avalanches is the heather-surrounded wreckage of a miner's cabin. The trail emerges into grass and flowers of the cirque, 10½ miles, 4200 feet, and fades away. The views of Goode are better than ever and Logan's walls are close above the amphitheater.

Air view of Park Creek Pass: Mount Buckner, left; Mount Logan, right

LAKE CHELAN—STEHEKIN RIVER
North Cascades National Park

48 PARK CREEK PASS

Round trip to pass 16 miles
Allow 3–4 days
High point 6100 feet
Elevation gain 3900 feet

Hikable mid-July through
September
USGS Goode Mountain and Mt.
Logan
Park Service backcountry use
permit required for camping

A wild and alpine pass on the Cascade Crest between the 9000-foot summits of Mt. Buckner and Mt. Logan, dividing snow waters flowing east to the Stehekin River and Lake Chelan and snow waters flowing west to the Skagit River and the Whulj (the name by which the original residents knew "the saltwater"). The pass and its surroundings rank among the scenic climaxes of the North Cascades National Park. A base can be established at Buckner Camp for roaming, or a one-way trip made over the mountains from lowlands east to lowlands west. Keep in mind that there is no camping in the alpine areas around the pass. From the last permitted camp in Park Creek it is 5 miles, with a 2000-foot climb, over and down to Thunder Basin Camp.

Travel 18½ miles from Stehekin (Hikes 45 and 46) to Park Creek Campground and trailhead, elevation 2300 feet.

The trail switchbacks steeply from the Stehekin into the hanging valley of Park Creek, then goes along near the stream through forest and occasional open patches with views up to Goode Ridge. At 2 miles, 3200 feet, is a two-site designated camp and a footlog crossing of the creek. Beyond here the grade gentles, continuing mostly in trees but with openings that give looks to Park Creek Ridge. At 3 miles is an obscure junction with a rough-and-sketchy climbers' route to 7680-foot Goode Ridge and broad views; the scramble is for experienced hikers only, but well worth the effort.

Crossing numerous creeks in green avalanche tracks, views growing of high peaks, the trail ascends gradually to 4000 feet, 4½ miles. Now the way leaves the main valley of Park Creek, which falls from the glaciers of Mt. Buckner, and traverses and switchbacks steeply into a hanging side-valley, gradually emerging into parkland. At 7 miles, 5700 feet, the trail flattens out in a magnificent meadow laced by streams and dotted by clumps of alpine trees, the view dominated by the north wall of 8200-foot Booker Mountain.

A final wander in heather and blossoms leads to the rocky, snowy defile of 6100-foot Park Creek Pass, 8 miles from the Stehekin road.

In order to preserve the fragile meadows, camping is not permitted in the area near the pass; however, fair basecamps for exploration are located in the forest at 5 miles (Buckner Camp) and 2 miles west of the pass in Thunder Basin.

For one wandering, with grand views of Buckner, Booker, Storm King, and Goode (tallest of all at 9160 feet, third-highest non-volcanic peak in the Cascades), find an easy, flowery route to the ridge southeast of the pass, overlooking the head of Park Creek. For another, descend west from the pass about ½ mile, leave the trail, and contour meadows and moraines to a jaw-dropping vista of the giant Boston Glacier and great peaks standing far above the valley of Thunder Creek.

If transportation can be arranged, a one-way trip can be made on down Thunder Creek to Diablo Lake (Hike 32).

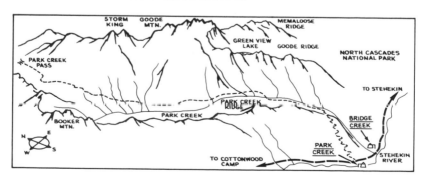

49 HORSESHOE BASIN (STEHEKIN)

**Round trip from Cascade River
  road 18 miles**
Allow 3–4 days
**Elevation gain 3000 feet in, 1800
  feet out**
Hikable July through October
**USGS Cascade Pass and Goode
  Mountain**
**Park Service backcountry use
  permit required for camping**

**Round trip from Cottonwood
  Camp 8 miles**
Hiking time 5 hours
Elevation gain 2000 feet

Nine or more waterfalls tumble to the meadow floor of this cliff-ringed cirque. Above are glaciers on Sahale and Boston Peaks, both nearly 9000 feet, and the spires of Ripsaw Ridge. Wander the flowers and rocks and bubbling streams. The basin is well worth a visit in its own right, and

Glory Mountain, left, Trapper Mountain, right, from mine in Horseshoe Basin

makes a splendid sidetrip on the cross-mountain journey described in Hike 50.

The basin trail can be reached either from the west side of the Cascades or the east. For the west approach to the junction, ascend to Cascade Pass (Hike 44) and descend 3 miles into the Stehekin valley. For the east approach to the junction, travel to the end of auto road at Cottonwood Camp, 2800 feet, and walk the abandoned mining road 2 miles (Hikes 45 and 46).

At an elevation of 3600 feet on the Stehekin River trail, the old mining road (dating from the 1950s) switchbacks sharply in a rockslide, climbing around and up the mountainside to enter the hanging valley of Basin Creek. At 1½ miles the way emerges from brush and flattens out amid boulder-strewn meadows, 4200 feet. Impressive looks upward from flowery knolls to ice and crags, and a magical view and sound of white water on the glacier-excavated walls.

The old road continues ½ mile upward across the sloping floor of the basin to the Black Warrior mine tunnel at 4800 feet, close under the froth and splash of the falls. The Park Service has worked in the mine to make explorations safe; bring a flashlight. Hours can be spent roaming the basin, enjoying.

Experienced off-trail hikers can go higher. Cross the creek a short way below the mine and scramble brushy slopes, amid small cliffs to the right of the vertical walls, into the upper cirque of Horseshoe Basin. The ascent is not easy but doesn't require the ropes and other gear of mountain climbers; traces of an old miners' trail may be found, simplifying progress. Once on the high shelf under Mt. Buckner and Ripsaw Ridge the way is open for extended explorations, always looking down waterfalls to the lower basin and out to peaks beyond the Stehekin.

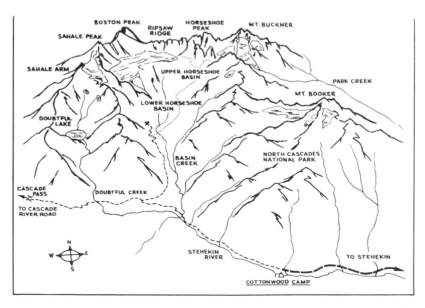

50 LAKE CHELAN TO CASCADE RIVER

One-way trip from Cottonwood
Camp to Cascade River road 9
miles
Hiking time 6 hours
High point (Cascade Pass) 5400
feet
Elevation gain 2600 feet
Hikable mid-July through mid-
October
One day
USGS Goode Mountain and
Cascade Pass

One-way Boy Scout hike from
Prince Creek to Cascade River
50 miles
Allow at least 6 days
Elevation gain 5900 feet, loss 2600
feet
Park Service backcountry use
permit required for camping

A classic and historic cross-Cascades route from the Columbia River to
Puget Sound. The trip can begin from either side of the range, but for a
well-ordered progression of soup, salad, main course, and finally dessert
(rather than the reverse) the approach from the east is recommended.
The journey can be a quick-and-easy 9 miles or, by starting at Prince
Creek, a Boy Scout "50-mile hike."

Voyage Lake Chelan, elevation 1098 feet (Hike 45).

Begin the 50-mile hike at Prince Creek, then walk the quiet road from
the Stehekin boat landing to Cottonwood Camp, 2800 feet, 23 miles from
Stehekin and the end of automobile traffic. Hikers who don't need a
merit badge may ride the shuttlebus this far (Hike 46).

At Cottonwood Camp the way emerges from woods into avalanche
greenery and goes along the valley bottom, with views of ridges above,
to the grassy-and-bouldery avalanche fan at the crossing of Basin
Creek, 3100 feet, 1½ miles from Cottonwood; campsite here. In another

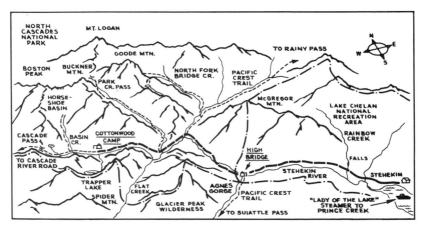

Stehekin valley and McGregor Mountain from Cascade Pass trail

¾ mile, at 3600 feet, is the junction with the route into Horseshoe Basin (Hike 49).

Excellent trail climbs an enormous talus to Doubtful Creek, 4100 feet, ¾ mile from the Horseshoe Basin junction. The ford can be difficult and extremely dangerous in high water, and falls above and below forbid any easy detour. Now the trail rises into a hot slope of slide alder, ascending in 12 gentle switchbacks to the crest of the wooded ridge above Pelton Basin and views. In the basin at 4820 feet, 5 miles, the Park Service has installed wooden tent platforms to allow camping in meadows without destroying them. This is a superb base for easy explorations.

A short mile more leads to 5400-foot Cascade Pass and broader views. A supertrail descends 3¾ miles to the end of the Cascade River road, 3600 feet (Hike 44).

51 CHELAN SUMMIT TRAIL

One-way trip 38 miles
Allow 5–9 days
High point 7400 feet
Elevation gain about 10,000 feet

Hikable early July through
September
USGS South Navarre, Martin
Peak, Prince Creek, Oval Peak,
Sun Mountain, Stehekin

A miles-and-miles and days-and-days paradise of easy-roaming ridges and flower gardens and spectacular views westward over the deep trench of (mostly unseen) Lake Chelan to the main range of the Cascades. Snow-free hiking starts earlier, and the weather is better, than in the main range, which traps many winter snows and summer drizzles. Only twice before the final plunge does the trail dip as low as 5500 feet, in forest; eight times it climbs over passes or shoulders, the highest 7400 feet; mainly it goes up and down (a lot) through meadows and parkland on the slopes of peaks that run as high as 8795-foot Oval Peak, in the Sawtooth Group. Good-to-magnificent camps are spaced at intervals of 2 to 3 miles or less. Sidetrips (on and off trails) to lakes, passes, and peaks are so many that one is constantly tempted; for that reason a party should allow extra days for wandering.

The trail can be sampled by short trips from either end or via feeder trails from Lake Chelan on one side or the Methow and Twisp Rivers on the other. (For examples of the latter, see Hikes 53 and 55.) The perfect dream trip is hiking the whole length to Stehekin, but this requires either a two-car switcharound or a very helpful friend to do drop-off and pickup duty. Further, the road routes range from rude to disgusting. Some cars simply can't get there. Most parties thus settle for a nearly perfect dream trip that starts on a feeder trail from the lake and uses the *Lady of the Lake* (Hike 45) to handle the drop-off and pickup.

Thanks (no thanks) to the maddening motorcycles still permitted on the south end of the Summit Trail, experienced hikers will opt to bypass part of it on the rough and steep Summer Blossom Trail (Hike 52). Beginners, however, had best take ear plugs and dust masks and sedatives and set out where the wheels do—notebook in hand to compose the letter of complaint that will be sent—after the trip to a Congressman, with a copy to the Forest Service.

The Summit Trail has two trailheads other than the Summer Blossom alternate—from South Navarre Campground and Safety Harbor Creek. Because the final 2 miles of road to the former generally are too rough for a family car, the latter is described here.

Drive the North Shore Road from Chelan past Manson and turn right on Grade Creek road, signed "Antilon Lake" and at this point becoming road No. 8200. At 36 miles from Chelan go left on road No. (8200)150, signed "Safety Harbor Trailhead," and continue 2 miles to the end and trailhead, elevation 4400 feet.

View from side of South Navarre Peak

Safety Harbor trail No. 1261 follows an abandoned pipeline a scant 2 miles and then turns uphill. At 4 miles, 5700 feet, it intersects Chelan Summit Trail No. 1261, which has just descended 600 feet in 3 miles from the South Navarre Campground. The Summit Trail now climbs to meadows of Miners Basin (5 miles) and a ridge crest. A traverse above headwater meanders of Safety Harbor Creek in Horsethief Basin leads to the 7400-foot pass (6½ miles) to East Fork Prince Creek. At the pass is a junction with the Summer Blossom Trail, which has come here in 6 miles from the road.

The way drops a bit to the broad meadow basin of the East Fork and makes a big swing around it, across the foot of 8321-foot Switchback Peak (an old trail switchbacks nearly to the summit) to the 7120-foot pass (8 miles) to Middle Fork Prince Creek. Down and around another wide parkland, at 10 miles are the junction with the Middle Fork Prince Creek trail and a basecamp for sidetrips to Boiling Lake and Hoodoo Pass and all.

(The Middle Fork Prince Creek trail is the best feeder for a tidy loop. Have the *Lady* drop you at Prince Creek, on the uplake side [Hike 45], and gain 5500 feet in 12 miles. Camps at 4, 6, and 8 miles from the lake.)

The trail climbs to Chipmunk Pass, the 7050-foot saddle (11½ miles) to North Fork Prince Creek, and here enters the Lake Chelan—Sawtooth Wilderness, the end of motorcycles. It descends to a 5560-foot low point in forest (14 miles) and climbs to flowers again and the 7400-foot pass (18½ miles) to East Fork Fish Creek. In odd-numbered years, sheep that have been driven up Buttermilk Creek here graze northward, devouring the flowers and fouling the water. (That's *another* letter for you to write to your Congressman, with a copy to the Forest Service.)

A short, steep drop leads to a 6800-foot junction with the trail to Fish Creek Pass (the sheep route). From a camp here, sidetrips include a stroll to larch-ringed Star Lake beneath the great wall of Star Peak and scrambles to the summits of 8690-foot Star Peak and 8392-foot Courtney Peak. On the other hand, if camp is made after a meadow traverse to Twin

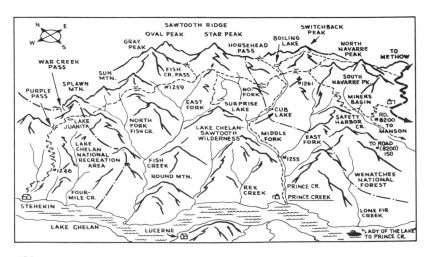

Chelan Summit Trail near the headwaters of Safety Harbor Creek

Springs Camp in Horseshoe Basin, there are sidetrips to Tuckaway Lake, Gray Peak, and Oval Lakes.

The way ascends to the 7400-foot pass (22 miles) to North Fork Fish Creek, descends to 5520-foot woods (24½ miles), and climbs through gardens (camps off the trail, near Deephole Spring) to a 7250-foot pass (27½ miles) to Fourmile Creek. A descent and an upsy-downsy traverse lead to Lake Juanita, 6665 feet, 30 miles. The quick and terrific sidetrip here is to Boulder Butte, 7350 feet, one-time lookout site.

At 30½ miles is 6880-foot Purple Pass, famous for the gasps drawn by the sudden sight—5800 feet below—of wind-rippled, sun-sparkled waters of Lake Chelan, seeming close enough for a swandive. Hundreds of switchbacks take your poor old knees down Hazard and Purple Creeks to Stehekin, 38 miles, and the ice cream.

52 SUMMER BLOSSOM TRAIL

One-way trip to Chelan Summit
Trail 6 miles
Elevation gain 1800 feet in, 600
feet out

Round trip to North Navarre
viewpoint 5 miles
Hiking time 4 hours

High point 7850 feet
Elevation gain 1400 feet
Hikable mid-July through
September
One day or backpack
USGS South Navarre Peak,
Martin Peak

You say horse manure ruins your lunch? Motorcycles convince you there's a bright side to nuclear extinction? The south end of the Chelan Summit Trail weakens your belief in a Benign Creation? Is that what's bothering you, Bunky? Be of good cheer! Take the Summer Blossom Trail! Sniff the blossoms in peace on a "hikers only" trail! Enjoy the horizons unobstructed by the blue haze of exploding hydrocarbons! But note that this Utopia is for experienced backpackers, not beginners.

The ancient sheepherders' driveway, recently resurrected and lovingly renamed, parallels the Summit Trail for 6 miles, traversing gardens in sky-high views. There are two problems. The first is driving to the trailhead. The second is that the path is steep, in part rough, and in part hardly there at all. However, if the trailhead can be reached, the route provides a magnificent day hike to the top of North Navarre Peak, or a gorgeous 2- or 3-day round trip, or the start of a week-long journey along the Sawtooth Ridge and on down to Stehekin.

The road—if such a cliffhanger deserves the name—often is impassable to ordinary passenger cars; before setting out, check at Chelan Ranger Station. One approach is via Grade Creek road (Hike 51); however, the 2 miles beyond Safety Harbor trailhead to South Navarre Campground are sporty for jeeps but a misery for the Family Circus Wagon, though the 2 final miles from the campground to the Summer Blossom trailhead are quite decent. The least bad approach is from the Methow Valley. From Pateros on the Columbia River drive the Methow

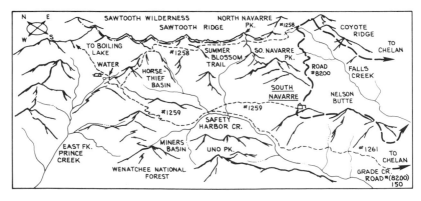

Summer Blossom Trail on side of North Navarre Peak

Valley Highway 17 miles toward Twisp. Just before crossing the Methow River the seventh time turn left on Gold Creek Road. In 1 mile turn left on road No. 4340 and in 1 mile more left again on road No. 4330, which begins as well-graded gravel, the better to inveigle you, my dears. At about 5.5 miles from this junction is another; go right, following the sign, "Cooper Mountain Road 7." These 7 miles grow steeper, narrower, slipperier, spookier. The junction with Cooper Mountain Road is in a scenic parkland saddle on the divide between the Methow River and Lake Chelan. Turn right 9 miles on road No. 82, sliced just far enough into the flowery sidehill for two hikers to walk side by side comfortably. At 23.5 miles from the Methow Valley Highway is Summer Blossom trailhead, elevation 6440 feet.

The wheelfree, horse-free, narrow, sometimes meager trail ascends "Narvie Basin," as oldtimers pronounce "Navarre," then the ridge of North Navarre Peak. At about 1½ miles it rounds a knob, crosses fields of boulders and blossoms of arid-land flowers, and at about 2½ miles tops out on a 7850-foot shoulder that is a quick stroll from the summit of North Navarre, 7963 feet; on shoulder as on summit, there are views from snow giants of the Cascade Crest to the scorched earth of the Columbia Plateau. For a day hike, this is a most spectacular turnaround.

The trail continues to be steadily and wildly scenic as it loses about 400 feet in tight switchbacks and a balcony traverse under a cliff, then roams open meadows on the very crest of Sawtooth Ridge and swings around the slopes of a 7751-foot peaklet. At 4½ miles it drops to a tiny basin with water and luscious camps in early summer (only), then ascends a bit and contours to a junction with the Summit Trail at the 7400-foot pass between Horsethief Basin and East Fork Prince Creek headwaters, attained at 6 miles from the Summer Blossom trailhead.

For the first campsite with guaranteed water (providing the sheep haven't been there first) go another ½ mile down into the lush basin at the headwaters of the East Fork.

September frost on Foggy Dew Creek

LOWER METHOW RIVER
Unprotected area

 FOGGY DEW CREEK

Round trip to Sunrise Lake 13 miles
Allow 2 days
High point 7200 feet
Elevation gain 3700 feet

Hikable mid-July through September
USGS Hungry Mountain and Martin Peak

The name has magic for those who love the folk song, and the scene has more. Maybe the stiff climb of 3700 feet doesn't usually stir the poetry in a hiker's soul, but the loud waters of Foggy Dew Creek do, and the lake in a horseshoe cirque amid meadows, cliffs, and parklike larch and alpine firs. Try it in late September when the larch has turned to gold. However, since hunters are here then, maybe you'd prefer the midsummer solitude, caused in no small measure by the fishless condition of the shallow lake. A party could spend many days happily here, exploring the sidetrails on both sides of the divide, and, as well, the Chelan Summit Trail (Hike 51), to which this trail leads.

From Pateros on the Columbia River drive the Methow Valley Highway 17 miles toward Twisp. Just before crossing the Methow River for the seventh time, turn left on a narrow country road 1 mile to a Forest Service sign. Turn left on road No. 4340. (From Twisp drive 15 miles toward Pateros. Just before crossing the Methow River, for the third time, turn right on a narrow country road. In 1.5 miles turn right at the abovementioned Forest Service sign.) Whichever way you reach it, from this sign drive North Fork Gold Creek road No. 4340 for 5 miles and turn left on road No. (4340)200. At 9.1 miles are the road-end and trailhead, elevation 3490 feet.

Foggy Dew trail No. 417 starts in selectively logged (all the big pines) forest, climbs steadily, and at 2½ miles passes Foggy Dew Falls, something to sing about. At 3½ miles the valley and trail turn sharply right. At 4 miles cross a small tributary and at 5 miles come to a junction with Martin Peak trail No. 429 and the end of the motorcyclists.

At 5½ miles, 6700 feet, steepness lessens and the path ascends moderately in ever-expanding meadows. At 6 miles reach Merchants Basin and a junction with a way trail to Sunrise Lake. From here the Foggy Dew trail to the Chelan Summit is seldom traveled and hard to find in the meadow; a USGS map is essential to further navigation.

The well-used Sunrise Lake trail climbs ½ mile to the shores at 7200 feet, 6½ miles from the road. Explorations abound, but campsites are limited and badly eroded, and the lovely water may be contaminated by horses; better to camp in Merchants Basin.

For a different way back, adding an extra 2 miles, 1200 feet, more meadows, and another lake to the round trip, at the trail junction in Merchants Basin find the seldom-used trail climbing toward an unnamed pass to the north. The tread is hidden in vegetation. Near the pass veer off to the right and in 1½ miles reach Cooney Lake and return to the Foggy Dew trail by trail No. 429.

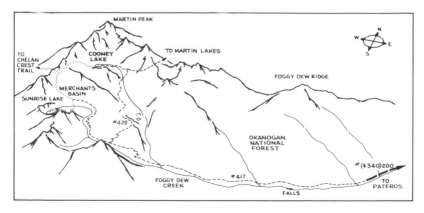

Cooney Lake and Switchback Mountain

54 COONEY LAKE

Round trip 16 miles
Hiking time 10 hours
High point 7241 feet
Elevation gain 3750 feet

Hikable mid-July through
September
One day or backpack
USGS Martin Peak

The jewel of the Sawtooths, that's what many hikers call Cooney Lake, located at the edge of timberline, the shores sprinkled with lovely larch trees, the waters mirroring the towering cliffs of the cirque.

Drive to Foggy Dew trail No. 417 (Hike 53), elevation 3490 feet.

Ascend the Foggy Dew trail 5 miles to a junction, 6000 feet, and go right on Martin Creek trail No. 429. The way switchbacks upward 3 miles, gaining 1200 more feet, crossing two forks of Foggy Dew Creek. At 8 miles from the road the Martin Creek Motorcycle Expressway on which you have been jaywalking goes right and a hiker-horse path crosses the creek, enters a meadow, and reaches the shore of Cooney Lake, 7241 feet.

To help the Forest Service revegetate the shore, don't camp here, but continue on the trail above the left side of the lake to areas less brutalized.

For extra stimulation, add a loop trip to the basic trip, and a sidetrip from the loop to Sunrise Lake (Hike 53). Stay on the trail from Cooney Lake as it climbs over a low cliff on the south side, past a shallow (maybe dry) pond, and steeply switchbacks to an 8000-foot pass. Descend to Merchants Basin and proceed down the Foggy Dew trail, past the sidetrail to Sunrise Lake, to the starting point. The loop adds 3 miles and 1000 feet of elevation gain, plus the numbers for the sidetrip.

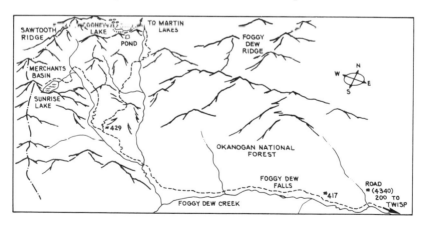

55 EAGLE LAKES—BOILING LAKE

Round trip 17 miles
Allow 2 days
High point 7600 feet
Elevation gain 2800 in, 700 feet out

Hikable July through September
USGS Martin Peak

Pretty Eagle Lakes under beetling crags. A 7590-foot pass across the Chelan Summit to Boiling Lake. A bushel of byways to meadow nooks. Easy-roaming routes to peaks with views over forests and sagebrush to ranches in the Methow Valley, over the Lake Chelan trench to ice giants of the North Cascades.

The "National Recreation Trail" (whatever that is) has been rebuilt smooth and wide, with banked corners. For the benefit of racing hikers? Galloping horses? Not at all. For the motorcyclists who burrowed into the state bureaucracy and—making sure to keep the plot from hikers—turned the former foottrail into a machine speedway. To avoid dust and danger and aggravation, it is recommended you do this trip in late June or early July when snowpatches still stop wheels but not feet. Take note of the mint of money the Forest Service spent to "improve" the trail for motorcycles, and the obviously costly maintenance. Note, too, that for the benefit of horsemen, who in the beginning were the earliest to do battle against the invasion by wheels, the Forest Service has installed at the trailhead a water system for horses, several corrals, and picnic tables. This is called "multiple use," or "something for everybody." For hikers it means dodging hot wheels and finding a safe place to pass horses. (Have *you* written *your* letter to your Congressman, with a copy to the Forest Service?)

Drive North Fork Gold Creek road No. 4340 (Hike 53) 6.6 miles to a junction. Turn left on road No. (4340)300 for 6 miles to Eagle Lake trail No. 431, elevation 4700 feet.

The first mile is fairly level, then a steady ascent begins. Pass the Crater Lake trail (Hike 56) and the Martin Creek trail (Hike 57). At 4½ miles, 6900 feet, a hiker-only sidetrail goes off left, dropping 200 feet in ½ mile to Lower Eagle Lake, good camping. The main trail proceeds to campsites near a small tarn and then, at 7000 feet, a short sidetrail to Upper Eagle Lake, 7 miles, 7110 feet.

At 7½ miles the main motorcycle raceway slices through the Sawtooth Ridge at Horsehead Pass, 7590 feet, between two 8000-foot peaks of the crest. The wheel-easy switchbacks descend 1 mile to Boiling Lake, not—as the name implies—a hot puddle in a sunbaked desert, but a cool pool in green meadows, with a number of widely scattered and pleasant campsites. (The "boiling" is bubbles of air rising from bottom mud.) The trail continues down a bit more to join the Chelan Summit Trail (Hike 51). Via that thoroughfare and its offshoots, or the old sheep trails from the lake, restless souls may wander to any number of flower gardens (early July is most colorful) and summit views.

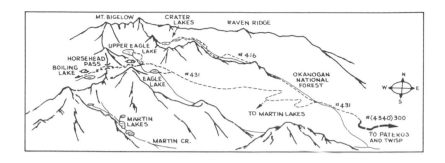

Boiling Lake

56 CRATER LAKES

Round trip 8 miles
Hiking time 5 hours
High point 6841 feet
Elevation gain 2100 feet

Hikable mid-June through
 September
One day or backpack
USGS Martin Peak

Oh yes, the Gold Creek scenery is terrific and the greenery is luscious, but the wheels wheels wheels razzing this way and that! The cavalry regiments beating the trails to dust! Who can handle it? Steel yourself, hiker, because in the middle of uproar an oasis of clear peace, a trail to two alpine lakes ringed by rugged peaks, surrounded by groves of neat trees and patches of pretty meadow. Motorcycles are prohibited—the trail is too steep for them. Horses are not—but the trail is too short and mean to please the heavy cavalry. So don't complain about the steepness. If the trail were improved it would become just another half-hour sidetrip for the wheel-spinners.

Drive to Eagle Lake trail No. 431 (Hike 55), elevation 4700 feet.

Hike the dusty Eagle Lakes razzerway No. 431 for a long ½ mile to a junction at about 4900 feet, just past Crater Creek. Go right on Crater Lakes trail No. 416, signed "No Motorcycles." The hiker is immediately struck by the fact the tread is covered not with inches of dust, as on ORV trails (roads), but needles. Ah, wilderness! In a long ½ mile (1 mile from the road) the path bridges Crater Creek. Several very steep stretches have been badly chewed up by the few horses which venture here. Otherwise the tread is in fair shape considering the gain of 2000 feet in 3 miles. The hiker will want to take the excuse of two viewpoints to pause, inhale deeply, and gaze across rolling hills to Methow ranches.

At 3¼ miles from the Eagle Lakes trail (4 miles from the road), 6814 feet, is the first of the two Crater Lakes. The horse camp is ¼ mile below the lake, but horse manure and hoof pits in campsites at the little meadow at the lakehead show that horses don't care.

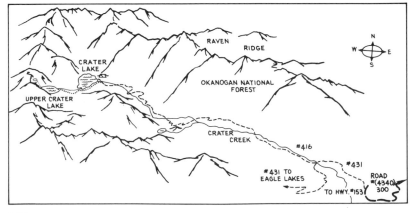

Upper Crater Lake

The upper Crater Lake has no formal trail. At the lower lake go right, around the shore, cross an inlet stream in the lakehead meadow, and continue to the second stream rushing down the mountainside. Cross it and follow the course up. A person who stays close to the tumbling water can't get lost but will have numerous windfalls to dodge. In ¼ mile, at 6969 feet, is the shallow upper lake. The ragged ridge to the south is a nameless spur of Mt. Bigelow. To the north is an extension of Raven Ridge. The surveyor found no horse souvenirs in the camps.

Lower Martin Lake

LOWER METHOW VALLEY
Unprotected area

 MARTIN LAKES

Round trip 14 miles
Hiking time 8 hours
High point 6800 feet
Elevation gain 2500 feet in, 500
  feet out

Hikable July through September
One day or backpack
USGS Martin Peak

Beneath the cliffs of 8375-foot Martin Peak nestle two small lakes, the shores lined with larch trees; late September, when the needles turn golden before falling, is an especially fine time for a visit. But the flowers of early July are nothing to sneeze at either, unless you're allergic.

Drive to Eagle Lake trail No. 431 (Hike 55), elevation 4700 feet.
Hike the Eagle Lakes Obstacle Course (you being one of the obstacles) to a junction at 2 miles, 5100 feet. Turn left onto Martin Creek Expressway No. 429, dropping 500 feet in a bit less than 1 mile to a crossing of Eagle Creek. Watch out for runaway motorcycles doing 20 mph.

In long switchbacks suitably banked for speeding, ascend Martin Creek valley, never near the creek and, thanks to a wonderful old-growth forest, with few views to the outside world. At about 6½ miles from the road is a junction, 6400 feet. Go right on Martin Lake trail No. 429A. See the sign, "No Motorcycles," and make a happy face. Then make a different face on stretches of steep tread torn up by motorcycles (don't blame the machines—they can't read). At 7 miles, 6729 feet, is the first Martin Lake. Settle in to enjoy the peace under the larches. However, before your trip check with the State Game Department on the bag limit for illegal motorcycles.

A way trail along the shore leads in a scant ¼ mile to the second lake.

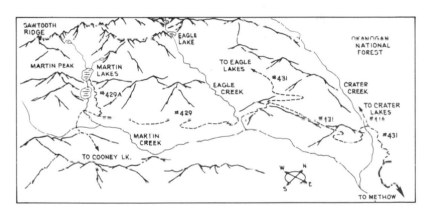

58 GOLDEN LAKES LOOP

Loop trip 23 miles
Allow 3 days
High point 8000 feet
Elevation gain 5500 feet

Hikable mid-July through
September
USGS Martin Peak

The Enchantment Lakes have gained wide and well-deserved fame—so much that the Forest Service has put forth a long list of restrictions to preserve the quality of the land and the recreational experience. Trembling on the brink of comparable fame is the Golden Lakes Loop—a route that goes through miles of meadows, passes five lakes and looks down to three others, and tops ridges with views from the Columbia Plateau to the Cascade Crest. The trip is a glory in summer, the grass lushly green and the flowers many-colored. In fall it's absolutely mystical, the larch trees turned to gold, giving the name by which this tour will become famous.

The hiker who takes the 3-day introduction will want to return for a week—for many weeks over many years. The first trip also will stimulate strong letters to Congressmen (copies to the Forest Service), asking how come the Enchantments are treated so tenderly as to exclude dogs and in this companion piece of wonderland motorcycles are permitted—more accurately say, officially encouraged.

The description here is counterclockwise; clockwise is just as good. As a complete loop the trip is not—presently—for beginners; a stretch of abandoned trail over a tricky pass is safe enough for travelers who know what they're doing but traverses terrain where a little mistake made from inexperience could be very bad.

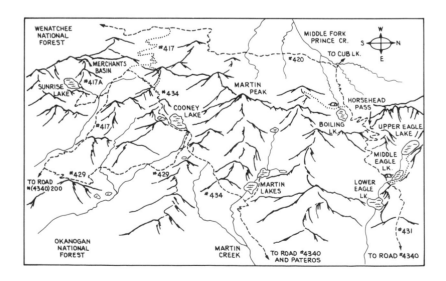

Drive to Eagle Lake trail No. 431 (Hike 55), elevation 4700 feet.

Start on this trail, at 2 miles passing Martin Creek trail (Hike 57), the final leg of the loop return. At 7 miles, 7110 feet, on a short spur from the main trail, is Upper Eagle Lake, with camps for the first night.

The second day's 6 miles, mostly above timberline, could keep a party of explorers happy for a week. Cross 7590-foot Horsehead Pass to Boiling Lake (Hike 55) and continue a mile down into open forest. At 9½ miles from the road is a junction with the Chelan Summit (Sawtooth) Trail (Hike 51), 6600 feet. Turn left on it, climbing back to meadows, passing nice campsites (if the water hasn't been fouled by sheep), to a 7100-foot saddle.

Contour from the saddle about ½ mile into the broad headwaters basin of East Fork Prince Creek. Look for tread, cairns, and/or horse manure heading off to the left and slanting up the meadows on the abandoned trail over Sawtooth Ridge, the route is incorrectly shown on the USGS map, correctly on the Twisp Ranger District Fire Map, as trail No. 417. The one and only real difficulty is finding the exact spot where the way goes from lush sidehill onto a vast boulder field on the slopes of "Switchback Peak," called this locally for generations because once the massive boulders had been levered apart to create the switchbacks, there couldn't ever be any problem finding the trail. Maintenance has been next to nothing in the near-century since sheepherders completed the engineering feat; some rocks have fallen onto the tread; so take it easy and don't stumble.

The switchbacks lead to a 7400-foot high point on the shoulder of the 8000-foot peak, tremendously scenic. The way sidehills above Merchant Basin to the ridge above Cooney Lake. (Steep snow here may force the unequipped to turn around or die.) Switchbacks drop to a campsite bench near the upper end of Cooney Lake (Hike 54), at 7241 feet.

The third day is mostly downhill. From Cooney Lake follow the outlet stream a few hundred feet to a junction with the Martin Creek trail. The right fork descends to the Foggy Dew trail; take the left, switchbacking down into forest and a junction with the sidetrail to Martin Lakes (Hike 57). Stay with the Martin Creek trail down to the crossing of Eagle Creek and up the 500 feet to the Eagle Lake trail, reached at a point just 2 miles from the trailhead.

Headwater basin East Fork Prince Creek

59 LIBBY LAKE

Round trip 11 miles
Hiking time 6 hours
High point 7618 feet
Elevation gain 3100 feet

Hikable July through September
One day or backpack
USGS Buttermilk Butte, Martin Peak

Massive rockslides dramatically ring the lake on three sides. On the fourth are giant larch trees that turn golden in fall. A connoisseur might judge the scene not quite as beautiful as the nearby Oval Lakes—unless he brought his nose into the evaluation, since the Ovals typically entertain up to half a hundred horses a weekend, while Libby rarely sees a horse wading out from its shore and letting a souvenir drop. The reason is that the trail is so steep in places as to be a notorious horse-killer. However, lest hikers rejoice to excess, the Forest Service plans to rebuild the trail to horse standards when funds can be found.

Drive Highway 153 from the Columbia River toward Twisp. Just 1.2 miles east of Carlton turn south (left) on the county road signed "Libby Creek." At 2.7 miles go left on road No. 43, signed "Black Pine Lake." At 5 miles from the county road go left on road No. 4340, signed "Gold Creek." In another 1.4 miles go right on road No. (4340)700, then left on (4340)750, signed "Libby Lake," to the road-end and trailhead, about 8.5 miles from the county road, elevation 4600 feet.

Logging has messed up the start of Libby Lake trail No. 415. The route goes very steeply up a cat track to the old tread, which contours the ridge slopes and then, with some ups and downs (more ups than downs) levels off and enters the Chelan-Sawtooth Wilderness. In about 2½ miles the trail crosses North Fork Libby Creek to a pleasant camp. It climbs into a forest of pine and larch and glacier-polished slabs, at 5 miles passing remnants of a falling-down cabin. Several rocky stretches (undoubtedly why there are no horses to speak of) lie along the way to the shores of the lake, 7618 feet, 5½ miles from the road.

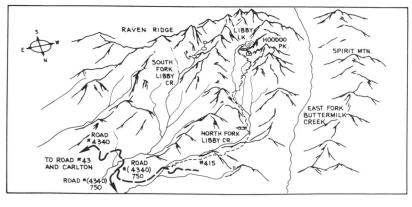

The shore has very little flat ground. At the outlet is a rock-filled dam, evidently built by farmers long ago and also forgotten long ago. (Golly knows what they had in mind. Irrigation?) A few hundred feet below the lake are some decent campsites.

Libby Lake

60 LOUIS LAKE

Round trip 10½ miles
Hiking time 5½ hours
High point 5351 feet
Elevation gain 2200 feet

Hikable mid-July through
October
One day or backpack
USGS Gilbert

Beneath one of the most rugged stretches of Sawtooth Ridge is Louis Lake, large for this part of the Cascades, lying under terrific cliffs of 7742-foot Rennie Peak on the left and a nameless 8142-foot peak on the

Louis Lake

right. So narrow is the gash of a valley that even in midsummer the sun touches the floor only a few hours a day.

Drive the Methow Valley Highway to Twisp, turn west on the Twisp River road 22½ miles, and just beyond South Creek Campground find the start of South Creek trail No. 401, elevation 3200 feet.

The trail ascends gently in sound of South Creek cascading down a slot canyon. At 2 miles, 3800 feet, is a junction. The main trail continues up South Creek another 5½ miles to the national park and a junction with Rainbow Creek trail. Go left on Louis Lake trail No. 428, dropping a bit to camps and a bridge over South Creek. South Creek Butte can be recognized by its red crest.

At about 3½ miles the path enters Louis Creek valley; a hiker has the dark suspicion he's entering a trap, a cul-de-sac with no escape through precipices. The trail contours high above Louis Creek with many ups and a few downs. At 4 miles, where the way parallels the stream, an opening appears in the otherwise unbroken expanse of high walls and the route proceeds through it to the lake, 5351 feet.

The setting is spectacular. On the far shore is a small, tree-covered island. The lake surface is largely choked with enormous masses of driftwood from gigantic winter avalanches. Camping at the lake is very limited and best not done at all; instead, use the sites several hundred feet before reaching the shore.

A second lake, tiny, is 1 mile away and 500 feet higher, which sounds like an easy amble, but it ain't, the access mostly over broad bad fields of big boulders. If determined to get there anyhow, find a trail of sorts that goes around a thicket of slide alder, then parallels the shore.

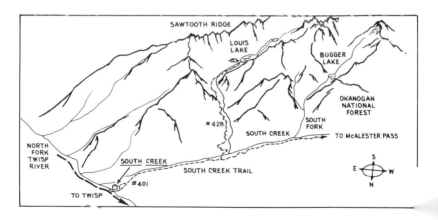

61 SCATTER LAKE

Round trip 9 miles
Hiking time 7½ hours
High point 7047 feet
Elevation gain 3900 feet

Hikable mid-July through
October
Backpack
USGS Gilbert

If you want a definition for "grueling," try this, and don't be fooled by the mere 4½ miles of hiking because they gain 3900 feet, unmercifully hot in the midday summer sun. Why do it, then? You'll know when you get there. From the cirque walls scooped in the side of 8321-foot Abernathy Peak the sterile brown talus, streaked with mineralized yellow and red, slopes to the shore of a stunning blue gem ringed by larches, their delicate green a striking contrast to harsh colors of the rock.

Drive the Methow Valley Highway to Twisp and turn west on the Twisp River road, signed "Gilbert," 22 miles (pavement ends 14 miles). After crossing Scatter Creek go off right on a sideroad 500 feet, passing a corral, to the start of Scatter Creek trail No. 427 (sign may be missing). Elevation, 3147 feet.

The route begins on a cat track dating from selective logging (all the big pines were selected). In ¼ mile the way becomes regular footpath. The first mile makes long, gentle switchbacks above the Twisp valley. The second mile traverses and switchbacks high above Scatter Creek. At 2½ miles the creek is close.

At this point whoever built the trail apparently got tired of switchbacks; from now on when the hill is steep so is the path. At 3½ miles cross the Scatter Lake fork of Scatter Creek and follow the right side of the stream (USGS map is wrong). At 4 miles is a delightful camp in sound of a waterfall. The trail climbs above the falls, levels out, passes a tiny tarn, and reaches the shore of Scatter Lake, 7047 feet. It was worth it. Numerous pleasant camps but little wood.

The highest point of the cirque wall is Abernathy. The summit is to the left of the point with a red cap.

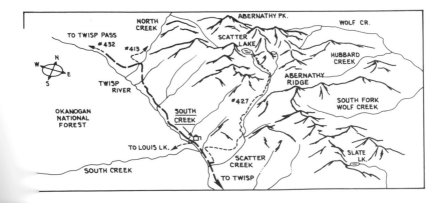

Larch trees and Scatter Lake

Dagger Lake from Twisp Pass

TWISP RIVER
Lake Chelan—Sawtooth Wilderness

62 TWISP PASS—STILETTO VISTA

Round trip to Twisp Pass 9 miles
Hiking time 6–8 hours
High point 6064 feet
Elevation gain 2300 feet
Hikable late June through October

One day or backpack
USGS Gilbert and McAlester Mountain
Park Service backcountry use permit required for camping at Dagger Lake

Climb from Eastern Washington forest to Cascade Crest gardens, glacier-smoothed boulders, dramatic rock peaks, and views down into Bridge Creek and across to Goode and Logan. Then wander onward amid a glory of larch-dotted grass and flowers to an old lookout site with horizons so rich one wonders how the fire-spotter could ever have noticed smoke. For a special treat do the walk in autumn when the air is cool and the alpine country is blazing with color.

Drive the Methow Valley Highway to Twisp and turn west on the Twisp River road, signed "Gilbert," 25 miles to the end. A short bit before the road-end is a large trailhead parking area, elevation 3700 feet.

The trail begins by ascending moderately through woods, with occasional upvalley glimpses of pyramid-shaped Lincoln Butte. At 2 miles are a junction with Copper Pass trail No. 426 and the last dependable water for a long, hot way. Cross the North Fork Twisp River, and continue fairly steeply on soft-cushioned tread to 3 miles; stop for a rest on ice-polished buttresses with views down to valley-bottom forest and up to the ragged ridge of Hock Mountain, above the glaciated basin of the South Fork headwaters. The trail emerges from trees to traverse a rocky sidehill, the rough tread sometimes blasted from cliffs. At about 4 miles the route enters heather and flowers, coming in a short ½ mile to a small stream and pleasant campsites. A final ¼ mile climbs to Twisp Pass, 6064 feet, 4½ miles, on the border of the North Cascades National Park.

The trail drops steeply a mile to Dagger Lake and 4 more miles to Bridge Creek and a junction with the Pacific Crest Trail.

For wider views ascend meadows north from the pass and look down to Dagger Lake and Bridge Creek and across to Logan, Goode, Black, Frisco, and much more.

Don't go away without rambling the crest south from the pass about ¼ mile to the foot of Twisp Mountain and a magical surprise—a hidden little lake surrounded by grass and blossoms and alpine forest, a mountain home.

The open slopes north of the pass demand extended exploration. And here is another surprise. Hikers heading in the logical direction toward Stiletto Peak will stumble onto sketchy tread of an ancient trail, fairly obvious the first mile, then less so. Follow the route up and down highlands, by sparkling creeks, to a green-shelf under cliffs of 7660-foot Stiletto Peak, a fairy place of meandering streams and groves of wispy larch. Then comes a field of photogenic boulders, a rocky ridge, and the 7223-foot site of the old cabin. Look north over Copper Creek to Liberty Bell and Early Winter Spires, northwest to Tower, Cutthroat, Whistler, Arriva, and Black, southwest to McGregor, Glacier, and Bonanza, and south to Hock and Twisp—and these are merely a few of the peaks seen, not to mention the splendid valley. Stiletto Vista, former lookout site, is only 2 miles from Twisp Pass, an easy afternoon's round trip.

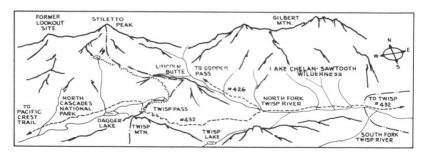

63 COPPER PASS

Round trip to pass 10 miles
Hiking time 6 hours
High point 6700 feet
Elevation gain 3000 feet

One day
Hikable July through mid-
October
USGS Gilbert and McAlester

The climb to the heathery pass is steep, but the color is worth it. Try the trip in July when glacier lilies and yellowbells are blooming, or in August for asters and cow parsnip and paintbrush and a few tucked-away gentians, or in late September when larch trees turn to gold.

The prospectors' trail of olden days connected the Twisp River to the Stehekin via Bridge Creek. Unused for decades, in 1981 and 1982 it was reopened to the pass by volunteers from the Sierra Club and Outward Bound. The trail down to Bridge Creek has not been brushed but can be found and used for a 3-day loop trip, returning via Twisp Pass (Hike 62). This alternative requires a backcountry permit for the North Cascades National Park, obtainable at the Twisp Ranger Station.

Drive the Twisp River road to the end, elevation 3700 feet (Hike 62). Hike Twisp River trail No. 432 for 2 miles to a junction just before crossing North Fork Twisp River (dwindled to a creek); go straight on trail No. 426, signed "Copper Pass." With more ups than downs the way follows the North Fork, mostly in woods. At 3½ miles cross the stream to a nice campsite, 5200 feet.

There's nothing now but up. In ¼ mile is a view of a double waterfall, and a bit farther, ruins of an old cabin. Scarcely deigning to switchback, the trail aims at the sky, partly in trees and partly in meadows.

At 6700 feet, 5 miles, is the sky—which is to say, Copper Pass, where herbaceous meadows yield to heather meadows. Day hikers may gaze down Copper Creek, across to the rocky ridge of Early Winters Spire, out to faraway ice-clad Goode Mountain, eat lunch, and go home satisfied.

Loopers can readily see the trail dropping steeply to green meadows at the head of Copper Creek. A bit of searching at the far edge of the boggy meadow may be needed to find the resumption of tread in forest. In about 4 miles from the pass the path intersects the Pacific Crest Trail. Follow it

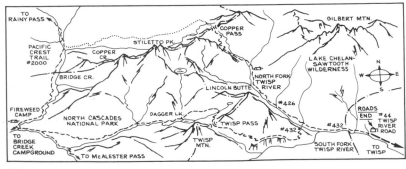

down Bridge Creek 1 mile to enter North Cascades National Park, then 1 more mile to Fireweed Camp, 3600 feet. From Fireweed, 4 long, steep miles climb to Twisp Pass, 6064 feet, and 4 shorter miles drop to the trailhead, completing a loop of 21 miles with an elevation gain and loss of 5500 feet.

Copper Pass

64 DRIVEWAY BUTTE

Round trip 8 miles	Hikable late May through
Hiking time 6 hours	September
High point 5982 feet	One day
Elevation gain 3100 feet	USGS Silver Star and Robinson
	Mountain

The former lookout site has views down the Methow Valley to ranches and towns and across to the Pasayten Wilderness, south to Gardner Mountain and the glaciers on Silver Star Mountain, and west to peaks of the Cascade Crest. There's a price to pay—sweat, much sweat. Be advised. Don't try the trip in the heat of day; the route has very little shade. Snow melts early on the south-facing slopes, making the hike possible in late May or early June when fields of sunflowers (balsamroot) are in full

Upper Methow valley from Driveway Butte

bloom. However, snow lingers in the high timber until middle or late June, halting a party not prepared to cope.

Of the three routes to Driveway Butte, two haven't been maintained for 20 years: trail No. 450, from Early Winters Campground; and trail No. 481, from Rattlesnake Campground, beginning with a difficult ford of the Methow River. The way described here is by the latter trail but from its other terminus, at Klipchuck Campground.

Drive the North Cascades Scenic Highway 20 east 12.6 miles from Washington Pass or 2.9 miles west from the Forest Service's Early Winters Information Center. Turn onto road No. (5310)300, signed "Klipchuck Campground," and drive 1 mile to the campground entrance; park here. A few feet back from the entrance find a gated forest road. Walk it about 500 feet to the start of Driveway Butte trail No. 481, elevation 2800 feet.

The trail sets out in a selective-logging area. The grade is moderate at first but soon slants steeply up open fields of bright yellow balsamroot with only an occasional shade tree. After climbing 2100 feet in approximately 1¾ miles (that seem like 3), the path levels a bit, enters a dense forest, and comes to a junction. The campsites here have no water after the snow melts in middle or late June. If snow covers the main trail, which forks left, take the right fork steeply to the top of a 5545-foot nameless butte. A window in the trees gives a spectacular view of Silver Star Mountain.

From the junction the angle of a main trail moderates but the tread grows rougher, at times is obscured by brush, and at about 3½ miles disappears. A few rock cairns lead across open slopes of Driveway Butte. Take careful note of the point where the tread vanishes; you'll want to find this point on your way home. Should you lose the trail on the way up, simply zig and zag to the summit. Marvel how completely the old horse trail has vanished on the slopes, only to reappear a hundred feet from the top.

The history of fire-watching from Driveway Butte began long, long ago with a platform in a tree. This was replaced in 1934 by a building on a 30-foot tower. In 1953 it was torn down and burned. Bits of glass and a scattering of rusty nails remain. So does the view.

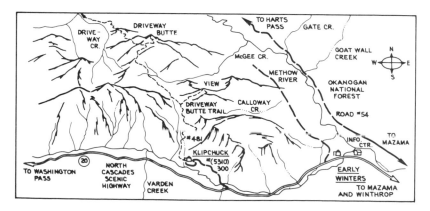

65   ABERNATHY PASS

Round trip 18 miles
Allow 2 days
High point 6400 feet
Elevation gain 3300 feet

Hikable July through October
USGS Mazama and Silver Star
Mountain

Finding the trails too peopled for your solitudinous tastes? Try Cedar Creek. Climb splendid forests, first in a narrow V valley and then in a broad U trough between Silver Star and Gardner Mountains, which do not present themselves in sweeping panoramas but through many peeking-type windows. Proceed to Abernathy Pass for the big picture. Or strike off through the open woods and get really lonesome and very high on slopes of the Big Kangaroo.

Drive the North Cascades Scenic Highway 20 west 3.5 miles from Early Winters Campground or east 13 miles from Washington Pass and turn onto road No. 200, signed "Cedar Creek Trail." At the road-end in .9 mile, turn right at a sign, "Trailhead," into a large gravel pit. Cedar Creek trailhead No. 476 is atop the bank to the left, elevation 3100 feet.

Though the trail starts 400 vertical feet higher than the creek, to stay above the wild torrent it gains 500 feet in a short 2 miles to Cedar Falls, a spectacular twin waterfall, the destination of most hikers, many of whom stay at the camp here overnight despite the danger to their hearing.

The way continues to climb steeply to keep dry. At about 3 miles is a window view of the craggy summit of North Gardner Mountain. At 4 miles the post-glacial notch is left behind and the U-shaped glacial trough entered, with a consequent flattening of the grade. The path crosses occasional aspen-dotted meadows that give looks at the impressive shoulders of Silver Star right and Gardner left, and far up the valley to a wall of mountains, part of the Abernathy Peak massif.

The pleasant forest walk is enlivened by creeks that may or may not be log-bridged and in snowmelt time may or may not be easy to get over. Campsites are scattered along the way, including one at West Fork Cedar Creek and another, the best and the last, a scant mile farther at Middle Fork, 7 miles, 5000 feet. (The old mile markers predate the Sandy Butte road, so subtract a mile.)

The valley head appears to be a cul-de-sac, no possible route through the solid wall of granite peaks. The 2 miles and countless switchbacks that climb 1400 feet to Abernathy Pass, 6400 feet, therefore seem a magic trick. The summit of the pass is a narrow cleft and the trail immediately drops to North Creek and the Twisp River. For views scramble the granite knobs west from the pass, on architecturally handsome ledges and slabs and buttresses, in picturesque pines and larches. The climax knob is ¾ mile, 7002 feet. Look north to Snagtooth Ridge and Silver Star Mountain and south across North Creek to Gilbert Mountain and pyramid-shaped Reynolds Peak, and back down the long valley whence you came.

The greatest hiking hereabouts is on paths beaten out by climbers. In

Cedar Creek Falls

open forests aromatic with Labrador tea and white rhododendron, and boggy glades dotted with insect-eating butterwort, then on steep heather meadows and rockslides, follow Middle Fork Cedar Creek to the south end of Kangaroo Ridge, or West Fork to the north end. Since this country has some of the most famous granite in the Cascades, watch out for Yellow Helmets chalking their fingers and snapping their carabiners.

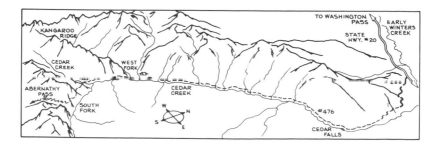

Mountain goats at Cutthroat Pass

EARLY WINTERS CREEK
North Cascades Scenic Highway (Corridor)

66 CUTTHROAT PASS

**Round trip from Cutthroat Creek
road-end to Cutthroat Pass 12
miles
Hiking time 6–8 hours
High point 6800 feet
Elevation gain 2300 feet
Hikable July through mid-
October
One day or backpack
USGS Washington Pass**

**One-way trip from Rainy Pass to
Cutthroat road-end 10½ miles
Hiking time 6–7 hours
High point 6800 feet
Elevation gain 1900 feet**

A high ridge with impressive views, among the most scenic sections of
the Pacific Crest Trail. If transportation can be arranged, one can start
at Rainy Pass and end at Cutthroat Creek, saving 400 feet of elevation
gain. However, because a short sidetrip to sparkling Cutthroat Lake
makes a refreshing rest stop, the trail is described starting from Cutthroat Creek.

Drive the North Cascades Scenic Highway 20 east from the Skagit
Valley over Rainy and Washington Passes, or west from the Methow
Valley 14 miles from Winthrop to Early Winters and 11 miles more to
Cutthroat Creek. Beyond the bridge turn right on the Cutthroat Creek
road 1 mile to the road-end and trailhead, elevation 4500 feet. The upper
regions are dry so have a full canteen.

The trail quickly crosses Cutthroat Creek and begins a gentle 1¾-mile ascent amid sparse rainshadow forest to a junction with the Cutthroat Lake trail. The 4935-foot lake (no camping) is ¼ mile away, well worth it.

The next 2½ miles climb through big trees and little trees to meadows and a campsite (no water in late summer). A final short 2 miles lead upward to 6800-foot Cutthroat Pass, about 6 miles from the road-end.

It is absolutely essential to stroll to the knoll south of the pass for a better look at the country. Cutthroat Peak, 7865 feet, stands high and close. Eastward are the barren west slopes of Silver Star. Mighty Liberty Bell sticks its head above a nearby ridge. Far southwest over Porcupine Creek is glacier-clad Dome Peak.

If time and energy permit, make a sidetrip 1 mile north on the Pacific Crest Trail to a knoll above Granite Pass and striking views down to Swamp Creek headwaters and across to 8444-foot Tower Mountain, 8366-foot Golden Horn, and Azurite, Black, and countless more peaks in the distance. This portion of the Crest Trail may be blocked by snow until mid-August.

From Cutthroat Pass the Crest Trail descends Porcupine Creek a pleasant 5 miles to Rainy Pass, the first 2 miles in meadows and the rest of the way in cool forest with numerous creeks. The trail ends a few hundred feet west of the summit of 4840-foot Rainy Pass.

The best camping is on flat spots near the head of Porcupine Creek, but none are close to water. At 3½ miles from Rainy Pass, ½ mile off the trail to the west, is a well-watered meadow camp.

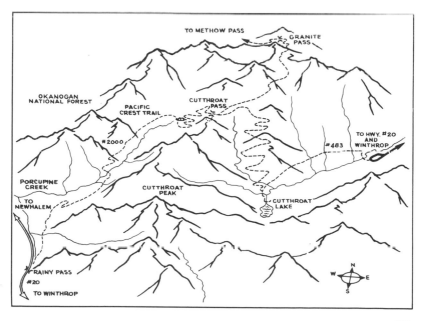

67 MAPLE PASS

Round trip to pass 8 miles
Hiking time 4½ hours
High point 6600 feet
Elevation gain 1800 feet

Hikable mid-July through mid-
 October
One day
USGS Mt. Arriva, McGregor
 Mountain, Rainy Pass

Lakes, little flower fields, small meadows, and big views sum up this delightful hike. The Forest Service built the trail to the pass, intending it to be a segment of the Pacific Crest Trail, only to discover what should have been obvious before, that the potential impact on fragile meadows by horse traffic would be disastrous. One certainly hopes it never will be completed down the far side of the pass (and therefore opened to horses).

Drive the North Cascades Scenic Highway 20 east from the Skagit Valley or west from the Methow Valley to Rainy Pass and park at the south-side rest area. Find trail No. 740 signed "Lake Ann-Maple Pass." Elevation, 4855 feet.

As is typical of the Pacific Crest Freeway, the trail was blasted wide enough for a cavalry charge. However, unless this does become part of the Crest Trail, horses will continue to be banned, as they now are, and that's a mercy for the meadows. Elevation is gained at the obnoxiously easy grade typical of the freeway. At 1½ miles, 5400 feet, is a spur to Lake Ann, destination of most hikers. The ½-mile path goes along the outlet valley, nearly level, by two shallow lakelets, around marshes, to the shore. Camping is prohibited within ¼ mile of the lake due to the dense population.

The main trail ascends across a large rockslide, by 2 miles getting well above Lake Ann. At 3 miles is 6200-foot Heather Pass; from a switch-back, look west to Black Peak, Lewis Peak, and the cirque of Wing Lake, out of sight under the peak. A way trail traverses steep hillsides of heather, snow, and boulders to Lewis Lake and Wing Lake; camping at the latter.

The main trail continues from Heather Pass, contouring over the top of

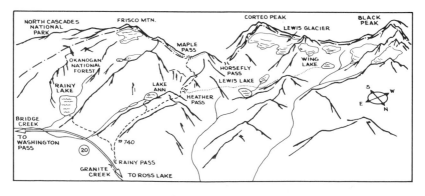

cliffs 1000 feet above Lake Ann to Maple Pass at 4 miles, 6600 feet, and there abruptly ends.

Boot-beaten tracks go left and right. The path west leads to a 6870-foot high point with close views of Corteo and Black Peaks. The path east leads to a shoulder of Frisco Mountain and views down Maple Creek and out toward icy-white Dome Peak, Spire Point, Mt. Resplendent, and Glacier Peak.

Corteo Peak from Maple Pass

GOLDEN HORN

Round trip 23 miles
Allow 2 days
High point 6900 feet
Elevation gain 2600 feet in, 600
  feet out

Hikable August through
  September
USGS Washington Pass

Several explanations are in order. First, three drainages are traversed on this spectacular section of the Pacific Crest Trail; designating it as "Early Winters" is arbitrary. Second, the hike is not to the summit of Golden Horn (Mountain), but to the Snowy Lakes, filling cirques scooped in the side of Golden Horn. Third—and not for us to explain—is why it is in an "unprotected area." When the North Cascades National Park was being proposed, pompous state and federal officials deigned to do a flyover and—at 10,000 feet—declared the area to be "not of national park caliber." Walk the ground. Make up your own mind.

Now, why do we call the trip "Golden Horn?" Because aside from

Upper Snowy Lake and Mount Hardy

rugged peaks and green meadows and groves of larch which turn gold in fall, the most distinctive feature of the region is the rock, which due to the complex mineralogy has a lovely pinkish-goldish hue. Geologists have dubbed it the "Golden Horn Granodiorite" and we think the rock alone makes the vicinity of national park caliber.

Drive North Cascades Scenic Highway 20 to Rainy Pass and park in the north trailhead area, elevation 4900 feet.

At a grade that refuses to exceed a horsey 10 percent, the two-horses-wide Crest Trail ascends through forest to big and bigger meadows. At 4 miles pass a campsite; at 5½ miles reach Cutthroat Pass, 6300 feet. The way continues up meadows and rockslides to a 6900-foot high point with a view of needlelike Tower Mountain and the golden horn of Golden Horn, then drops 600 feet to Granite Pass; snow may linger on the tread until August in this vicinity, at a steepness that will force hikers lacking ice axes to turn around. From the pass the freeway-size trail has been dynamited in cliffs a long 2 miles across the steep, hot slopes of Swamp Creek headwaters to a small stream, 6300 feet, in a meadow flat not yet recovered from the devastating impact of the construction crew which camped here just a single summer in the 1960s. See if you can find their horseshoe pits. Nevertheless, this is the place to camp.

A way trail climbs steeply ½ mile to Lower Snowy Lake, 6735 feet, and a bit more to Upper Snowy Lake, 6839 feet, miraculously located precisely in the summit of Snowy Lakes Pass. Thoughtless hikers and horsemen have contributed their share of damage to the acres of fragile meadows. Cowboys, leave your horses near the Crest Trail and walk; don't take them to dig post holes in the soft turf. Pedestrians, spread your sleeping bags by the Crest Trail, not on the heather or fragile meadows near the lakes.

The view from Snowy Lakes Pass is straight up the Golden Horn and Tower Mountain and out across Methow Pass to the spires of Mt. Hardy, above headwaters of the West Fork Methow River. The determined hiker can scramble onto slopes of Golden Horn Mountain, but the feldspar crystals are just as stunning throughout the batholith.

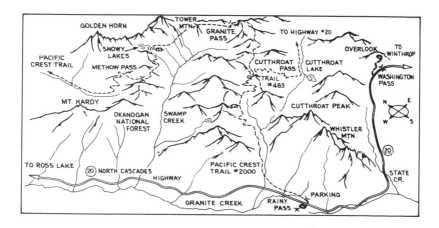

69   GOAT PEAK

Round trip 5 miles
Hiking time 6 hours
High point 7001 feet
Elevation gain 1400 feet

Hikable June through October
One day
USGS Mazama

A commanding view of the Methow Valley and the north face of Silver Star Mountain, the most beautiful and spectacular peak in the area. Most of the way is up a south slope, and all the way is hot and bone-dry, so start early and carry buckets of water.

Drive the North Cascades Scenic Highway 20 west 12 miles from Winthrop. Just before crossing the Methow River, go right on county road No. 1163 toward Mazama. At 6.2 miles turn right on road No. 52. From this intersection go another 3.7 miles and turn left on road No. 5225. At 8.3 miles from the Mazama road go right on road No. (5225)200 and at 11.2 miles reach a saddle and trailhead, elevation 5600 feet. To save ¼ mile of hiking, take the right-hand road; however, it is best to start at the trailhead, for the road is rough and the parking is difficult.

Goat Peak trail No. 509 takes off south, sometimes tree-shaded, sometimes in open, sparse meadows, sometimes on rocky ridges with great views. If often steep and rough, the tread is quite decently walkable as it switchbacks to the lookout building atop Goat Peak, 7001 feet.

Though 9 miles distant, 8901-foot Silver Star easily dominates the scene. North Gardner Mountain, 8956 feet, highest in the region, is a little to the south. Farther away are the spectacular peaks of Washington Pass. Northward rise the rolling, high ridges of the Pasayten Wilderness; this view of their south slopes makes them seem barren and unimpressive, very unlike the reality encountered by hikers.

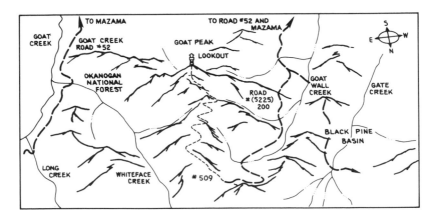

Silver Star Mountain from Goat Peak

Lost River near Eureka Creek

UPPER METHOW RIVER
Mostly unprotected area

 LOST RIVER

Round trip 8 miles
Hiking time 4 hours
High point 2700 feet
Elevation gain 400 feet in, 300 feet
    out

Hikable mid-May through
    October
One day or backpack
USGS Mazama and Robinson
    Mountain

A river-loud trail loiters along through forest and across rockslides to pleasant camps at the mouth of the legendary Lost River Gorge, a part of the Pasayten Wilderness, which is as wild as it was a century ago and is likely to remain so a century from now. Look all you want, and maybe even touch, if you dare.

Drive the North Cascades Scenic Highway 20 1.5 miles east of Early Winters Campground and turn left, cross the Methow River, and go .4 mile to the hamlet (post office, gas station, grocery) of Mazama and turn left again, upvalley on the Harts Pass road. Cross the Lost River and at 7.2 miles from Mazama turn right .3 mile to a parking lot, signed "Monument Valley Trail No. 484," elevation 2600 feet.

The wide and soft tread, next thing to flat, pokes along in forest 2 miles to the high point of 2700 feet. The next 2 miles are generally rough, in an alternation of trees and rocks. At about 3¼ miles (much too far up the valley) enter the Pasayten Wilderness. At 4 miles is the dramatic confluence of two gorges, Eureka Creek from the left, Lost River from the right. A sturdy bridge crosses Eureka Creek to choice campsites beside the Lost River at 2650 feet.

The usual plan is to loiter here for lunch or overnight, then loiter on back to the car. The trail does something perfectly awful—climbs 4600 feet up the hogback between the two canyons to 7300-foot Pistol Pass, and nary a drop to drink, then drops 2800 feet into Monument Creek, a tributary of Lost River. In the latter's gorge the hand of trail-constructing man never has set foot. Ascending the brutal path to hot-as-a-Pistol Pass is as recommendable as a Fourth of July picnic in Death Valley. However, it's worth huffing up ½ mile to a great view downriver towards Gardner Mountain.

At no point can a trail-walker see more than the awesome exit of the Lost River Gorge. The few doughty explorers who venture into its mysteries usually do so in late summer, when the river is low. They mostly wade, silently praying that no cloudbursts occur while they are in the chasm.

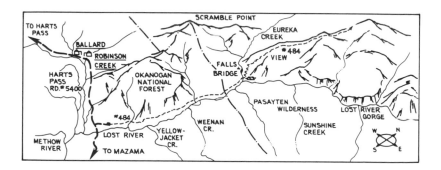

71 ROBINSON PASS

Round trip 18 miles
Allow 2 days
High point 6200 feet
Elevation gain 2700 feet

Hikable late May through
October
USGS Slate Peak, Robinson
Mountain, Pasayten Peak, Mt.
Lago, and Mazama

The geography here is not of the big glacier-monster crag sort characteristic of the North Cascades National Park, but spectacular it is—high, massive, shaggy ridges, naked and cliffy, reminding of Montana, and enormous U-shaped glacial-trough valleys, and awesome swaths of climax avalanches sweeping down from crests thousands of feet to bottoms and hundreds of feet up the other sides. Also, lovely streams rush through parkland forests. And among the greatest appeals, trips in what the local folk call the *"wilderness* Wilderness" are like taking a ride in a time machine back to the 1930s. Solitude! Though Robinson Creek is a main thoroughfare into the heart of the Pasayten Wilderness, and a favorite with horse people, most come in the fall hunting season. Summer is lonesome even on the main trail and on byways one can roam a hundred miles and maybe never see another soul.

Drive the Harts Pass road upvalley from Mazama (Hike 70). At 7 miles pavement ends. At 9 miles cross Robinson Creek and turn right into a small campground, parking area, and trailhead, elevation 2500 feet.

The trail follows the creek ¼ mile, then switchbacks a couple hundred feet above the water. At 1½ miles enter the Pasayten Wilderness and shortly cross a bridge over Robinson Creek. Partly in rocky-brushy opens, partly in forest of big Ponderosa pines, then smaller firs, the way climbs steadily, moderately, just short of 3 miles crossing a steel bridge over Beauty Creek, which waterfalls down from Beauty Mountain, at 4

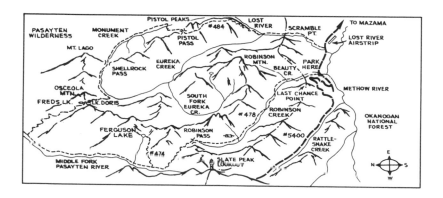

Trail near Robinson Creek

Trail bridge over Robinson Creek

miles recrossing Robinson Creek on a bridge. The avalanche country has been entered, wide aisles cut in the forest, huge jackstraws piled up; from here on the way is a constant garden.

At 6 miles are a log crossing of Robinson Creek, now much smaller, and Porcupine Camp, in the woods and unappealing except in a storm. To here, avalanche meadows have broken the forest. From now on strips of forest break the ridge-to-creek meadows. A nice camp is located in the first broad meadow above Porcupine; an even better in the second, at 6½ miles, 4900 feet, by the creek in a grove of large spruce trees; and a third just before Robinson Pass, in the trees 300 feet below the trail.

The trail sidehills through flower fields, rock gardens alternating with avalanche gardens, up to Robinson Pass at 9 miles, 6200 feet, a great broad gap through which the continental glacier flowed. Long-ago forest fires cleared the big timber and now the wildflowers blaze.

The pass is a trip in itself, but also is the takeoff for longer journeys. To begin, the open slopes above the pass invite easy roaming—to the left, up to big views from Peak 6935 and onward to Slate Pass, just 2 miles from

Robinson Pass and Slate Peak in clouds

Robinson Pass, and another mile to Slate Peak, or the other way on the long, lonesome heights of Gold Ridge; to the right, up to Peak 7720, and maybe along the ridge a mile to Devils Peak, or—climbers only—2 miles more to 8726-foot Robinson Mountain, the neighborhood giant.

If trail-walking is preferred, descend Middle Fork Pasayten River, through gaspers of avalanches from Gold Ridge, the most impressive series of swaths in the Cascades; 15 miles from the pass is Soda Creek, and in another 8 miles, Canada. The classic long loop of the region is: down the Middle Fork 6½ miles; up by Freds Lake to a 7100-foot pass, down by Lake Doris and around the headwaters of Eureka Creek, under Osceola, Carru, and Lago, three peaks between 8585 and 8745 feet, and up to Shellrock Pass, 7500 feet, 8 miles from the Middle Fork trail; 8½ miles down forests of Monument Creek and up by Lake of the Woods to Pistol Pass, 7100 feet; and 10¾ infamous miles down, down, and down, hot and thirsty, to the Lost River and out to the Methow road, reached at a point 2 miles from Robinson Creek. Total loop, 43 miles, elevation gain about 10,000 feet. Allow a week.

72 WEST FORK METHOW RIVER

Round trip 12 miles
Hiking time 6 hours
High point 3600 feet
Elevation gain 900 feet plus ups
and downs

Hikable late May through mid-
October
One day or backpack
USGS Robinson Mountain and
Slate Peak

Early in the season, when the highlands are of no use to anyone but skiers, is the happy time to walk this trail, sometimes beside the West Fork Methow River, always in sound of the roar, with look-ups through the trees to the country where the flowers will not appear for months. But they're already blossoming here.

Drive to Mazama (Hike 70) and proceed upvalley on the Harts Pass road 8.8 miles to a junction. Keep left on road No. (5400)060, signed "Riverbend Campground," .8 mile to the road-end and trailhead, elevation 2700 feet.

The trail crosses Rattlesnake Creek (yes, keep an eye out) and ambles up and down in forest and around and across giant rockslides. At about 2 miles it crosses Trout Creek on a log bridge and passes a campsite. At about 3 miles a delightful camp is located beside the river. At 4 miles the way ascends above the water and doesn't come back down for a mile. At 6 miles, 3600 feet, it leaves the river for good; time to go home.

The West Fork trail goes on, of course. At 7 miles, 4100 feet, it intersects the Pacific Crest Trail. Turning right (north) isn't recommended; Grasshopper Pass is better reached from Harts Pass. Turning left might be considered, because in that direction lie Methow Pass, Snowy Lakes Pass, and Golden Horn (Hike 68).

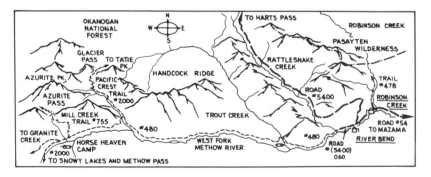

West Fork Methow River

Flower fields in Trout Creek valley
Trout Creek valley

73 TROUT CREEK

Round trip 6 miles
Hiking time 4 hours
High point 5425 feet
Elevation gain 100 feet in, 800 feet out

Hikable July through September
One day or backpack
USGS Slate Peak

When the meadows of the Harts Pass (very) highlands are engulfed in clouds, why fight the mists? Settle for a lower level, the (still quite) highlands, the vast meadows of South Fork Trout Creek. The trail doesn't get much maintenance, so it's rough and brushy in spots. In the meadows where the grass and flowers grow to a hiker's hips it can scarcely be seen or even found by probing feet. On a wet day this is an ideal place to test the claims of the manufacturers of those expensive rain pants.

Drive to Mazama (Hike 70) and proceed upvalley on the Harts Pass road. Abruptly ascend from the valley floor up the Big Hill, past Dead Horse Point. At about 18 miles from Mazama (just 2.3 miles short of Harts Pass) find Trout Creek trail No. 479, elevation 5425 feet.

The trail wanders up and down, seemingly without aim, the first ¼ mile. In the next ¼ mile it drops 250 feet from a rocky knoll. The next ¼ mile descends more moderately to a crossing of North Fork Trout Creek. The way continues down in woods, over several large boulder fields. At 2½ miles is the low point, 4600 feet, at the edge of meadowland.

The path now tilts slightly up, following the South Fork. In early July the tread might be findable another mile but by the end of the month, forget it. On the far side of the meadow are possible campsites.

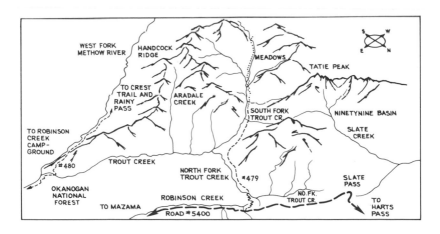

Azurite Peak and Grasshopper Pass

UPPER METHOW RIVER
Unprotected area

74 GRASSHOPPER PASS

Round trip 11 miles
Hiking time 6 hours
High point 7000 feet
**Elevation gain 1000 feet in, 1000
    feet out**

Hikable July through October
One day or backpack
USGS Slate Peak

Wide-open, big-sky meadow ridges with grand views of giant peaks
and forested valleys. The entire hike is above timberline, contouring hillsides, traversing gardens, and sometimes following the exact Cascade
Crest.

Drive to Mazama (Hike 70). Continue 20 miles upvalley to 6198-foot
Harts Pass. From the pass turn left on the Meadow Campground road 2

miles, keeping right at a fork, to the road-end and trailhead, elevation 6400 feet.

The Pacific Crest Trail immediately leaves the trees, going along an open slope below diggings of the Brown Bear Mine and above a pretty meadow. The first mile is a gentle ascent to the 6600-foot east shoulder of a 7400-foot peak. The way swings around the south slopes of this peak to a saddle, 7000 feet, overlooking Ninety-nine Basin at the head of Slate Creek, then contours 7386-foot Tatie Peak to another saddle, 6900 feet, and a magnificent picture of Mt. Ballard.

A moderate descent, with a stretch of switchbacks, leads around a 7500-foot peak. In a bouldery basin at 4 miles, 6600 feet, is the only dependable water on the trip, a cold little creek flowing from mossy rocks through a flower-and-heather meadow ringed by groves of larch. Splendid camps.

The trail climbs gradually a final mile to the broad swale of 6700-foot Grasshopper Pass. (Fine camps in early summer when snowmelt water is available.) But don't stop here—go ¼ mile more and a few feet higher on the ridge to a knob just before the trail starts down and down to Glacier Pass. The views are dramatic across Slate Creek forests to 8440-foot Azurite Peak and 8301-foot Mt. Ballard. Eastward are meadows and trees of Trout Creek, flowing to the Methow.

Each of the peaks contoured by the trail invites a sidetrip of easy but steep scrambling to the summit, and the wanderings are endless amid larches and pines and spruces, flowers blossoming from scree and buttress, and the rocks—colorful shales, slates, conglomerates, and sandstones, and an occasional igneous intrusion.

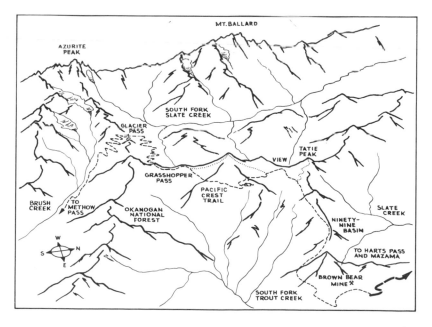

75   NINETY-NINE TRAIL

Round trip 9 miles
Hiking time 6 hours
High point 7000 feet
Elevation gain 700 feet in, 300 feet
  out

Hikable mid-July through
  September
One day or backpack
USGS Slate Peak

Here's a good and proper exercise for the pathfinder seeking to demonstrate his expertise with map and compass, to show what a keen nose he has for faint traces of ancient miners. If successful in following the long-abandoned trail, the reward is a lonesome camp on the green ridge overlooking Dicky Creek Basin. The only water will be from snowbanks. But with that and a jar of peanut butter and a harmonica, wilderness were Paradise enow.

Drive to Harts Pass and continue to the Grasshopper Pass trailhead (Hike 74), elevation 6400 feet.

Hike the Pacific Crest Trail south 1½ miles to a 7000-foot saddle directly above Ninety-nine Basin, for which the trail is named.

From this first saddle the Crest Trail drops slightly as it swings around Tatie Peak to a second saddle, 6900 feet, between Trout Creek and South Fork Slate Creek. Here the sport begins because the trail is not shown on the USGS map nor the Forest Service's Okanogan Recreation Map. (It is shown on the Service's Winthrop Fire Map but you, of course, will not have a copy of that.) Leave the Crest Trail here and go right, climbing a hundred feet or so up a shoulder of Tatie Peak. Find a steep, narrow path hacked in the cliffy mountainside and follow it over two rockslides, under the summit of Tatie Peak, to green slopes beyond. The trail then contours steep meadows interspersed with thickets of subalpine fir trees, some barely as tall as a hiker's hips but nonetheless nigh onto impenetrable. The tread is sometimes wide and plain, sometimes confused by a maze of animal walkways. A trail is not absolutely essen-

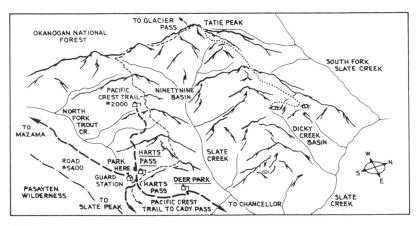

tial in this wide-open terrain but is distinctly easier traveling; when tread is lost, regaining it is worth the effort.

At 2 long miles from the Crest Trail the path crosses the ridge crest to a nice campsite and good turnaround point. For water, melt a pan of snow.

Alternately, proceed down the trail to Dicky Creek. The fire map shows the trail continuing to Ninety-nine Basin and looping back to Meadows Campground, near where you parked your car. Maybe so. But the loop is recommended only for those pathfinders seeking more glory than most hikers ever feel the need for. Miners' trails that survive decades in meadows vanish quickly in brushy forests, of which there are some on the loop, which is longer than it looks.

Mount Ballard from near first campsite

76   WINDY PASS

Round trip 7 miles
Hiking time 5 hours
High point 6900 feet
Elevation gain 500 feet in, 1000
  feet out

Hikable early July through
  October
One day or backpack
USGS Slate Peak and Pasayten
  Peak

In all the hundreds of miles of the Pacific Crest Trail in Washington, this ranks among the easiest and most scenic segments. The hike starts in meadows and stays high the entire way, contouring gardens thousands of feet above the trees of Slate Creek, magnificent views at every step.

Drive to Harts Pass (Hike 74) and turn right on the Slate Peak road about 1.5 miles to the first switchback and a small parking area at the trailhead, elevation 6800 feet.

If the trip is being done in early July, don't be discouraged if the road beyond Harts Pass is blocked by snow and the trail beginning is

Pacific Crest Trail in Benson Basin; Mount Ballard in distance

blinding-white; snow lingers here later than on any other portion of the hike, and mostly clear trail can be expected after a frosty start.

The Pacific Crest Trail gently climbs a meadow shelf the first ½ mile, contours steep slopes of Slate Peak, and drops into lovely little Benson Basin, with a creek and nice camps a few hundred feet below the tread. The way swings up and out to a spur ridge, contours to Buffalo Pass and another spur, and then descends above the gorgeous greenery of Barron Basin to 6257-foot Windy Pass and delightful camps in flowers and larch trees.

Sad to say, the wreckers have been here. Barron Basin is one of the most magnificent easy-to-reach glorylands in the Cascades, but it is mainly "private property" and the "owners" have raised havoc, gouging delicate meadows with bulldozers, dumping garbage at will. This hike is bound to convert any casual walker into a fierce enemy of the ultra-permissive federal mining laws, which make it next to impossible for the Forest Service to protect the land. Some of the desecration is very new but much is nearly a century old—note how long nature needs to restore ravaged meadows.

Sidetrips from the pass will make a person want the basin to be reclaimed for the public domain and placed within the Pasayten Wilderness, the boundary of which follows the divide, excluding the miner-mangled slopes to the west and the entire route thus far of the Pacific Crest Trail. Wander meadows north to the panoramas from 7290-foot Tamarack Peak, or walk the Crest Trail a short mile into Windy Basin, offering the best—and most heavily used—camps.

Views on the way? They start with Gardner Mountain, the Needles, Silver Star, Golden Horn, Tower Mountain, and especially the near bulks of Ballard and Azurite. Westerly, Jack and Crater dominate, but part of Baker can also be seen, and many more peaks. Easterly is the Pasayten country, high and remote.

Before or after the hike, take a sidetrip to the fire lookout on the 7440-foot summit of Slate Peak, formerly the highest point in Washington State accessible to automobiles; the road is now gated ¼ mile from the summit, and that's a help.

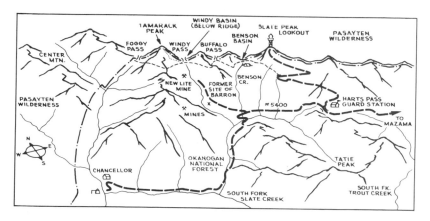

77 THREE FOOLS TRAIL

One-way trip from Castle Pass to
 Ross Lake 27 miles
Allow 3–5 days
High point 7000 feet
Elevation gain about 10,000 feet
Hikable mid-July through
 September
USGS Slate Peak, Pasayten Peak,
 Shull Mountain, Castle Peak,
 Skagit Peak, Hozomeen
 Mountain

One-way trip from Harts Pass to
 Ross Lake 54 miles
Allow 7–9 days

One-way trip from near Allison
 Pass (Canada) to Ross Lake 38
 miles
Allow 5–7 days

A classic highland wander from the Cascade Crest to Ross Lake, up and down a lonesome trail through some of the wildest valleys, ridges, and meadows in the range. A one-way trip is recommended, starting at Harts Pass (or near Manning Park headquarters in Canada) and ending at the lake. (See note on border crossings, Hike 100.) Special transportation arrangements are required: a drop-off at Harts Pass (or near Manning Park headquarters—see Hike 79); a pickup by boat from Ross Lake Resort (Hike 38)—though a party can, if desired; exit via the East Bank Trail.

Hike the Pacific Crest Trail (Hike 100) 27 miles from Harts Pass (or 11 miles from near Manning Park headquarters) to Castle Pass, elevation 5451 feet. Turn west on the Three Fools Trail (officially, Castle Pass trail No. 734), climbing steeply in forest, then meadows. At 3 miles, 6000 feet, enter a little basin with a welcome creeklet—the first dependable water since before Castle Pass, and the last for several more miles. Tread ascends from the basin, swings around a spur, descends meadows to a saddle, and climbs the crest to a 6534-foot knob that ranks among the most magnificent viewpoints of the region. Look north across the headwaters of Castle Creek to Castle Peak, Frosty Mountain in Canada, and Mt. Winthrop; look south across forests of Three Fools Creek to peaks along and west of the Cascade Crest; look in every direction and look for hours and never see all there is to see. The way drops from the knob and climbs ridge-top heather and parklands to 6 miles, 6400 feet, and a grandly scenic camp—but the only water, if any, is from snowmelt.

The trail angles down across a broad, steep flower garden, then switchbacks through avalanche-wrecked forest to Big Face Creek, beneath the impressive wall of Joker Mountain. (At 6½ miles is a tumbling creek; below the trail here is a campsite on a tiny, wooded shelf.) At 8 miles, 5200 feet, the path reaches the valley bottom. For a mandatory sidetrip, fight through a bit of brush and climb the open basin to a high saddle with views out to Hozomeen and the Chilliwacks and below to a snowy cirque lake draining to Freezeout Creek.

The trail goes gently downstream in trees to a crossing of Big Face Creek at 8¾ miles, 4840 feet, then turns right in a gravel wash to the ford. A possible camp here on gravel bars.

Three Fools Peak from Lakeview Ridge (Harvey Manning photo)

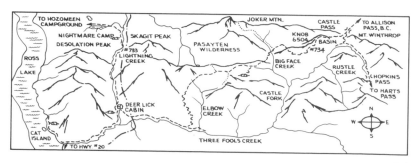

Weathered snag

A long climb begins up forest to avalanche greenery; when tread vanishes in the grass go directly uphill, watching for sawn logs. The ascent continues in trees, opens to meadows, and at 11½ miles, 6350 feet, tops out in the wide green pass, with broad views, between Big Face and Elbow Creeks. A sidetrail drops ¼ mile to a campsite and meandering stream in the glorious park of Elbow Basin. The main trail—tread missing for long stretches—contours and climbs north around the basin to a grassy swale (and a scenic camp, if snowmelt is available) near the ridge crest at 13 miles. Be sure to walk to the 6687-foot plateau summit of the ridge and views: east to the Cascade Crest; south to Jack Mountain; west to the Pickets, Chilliwacks, Desolation, and especially the nearby towers of Hozomeen; north into Canada.

The trail descends near and along the crest, with a look down to the tempting cirque of Freezeout Lake (accessible via a steep scramble), passing through a spectacular silver forest. A stern drop commences—

down and down hot and dry burn meadows and young trees. The mouth grows parched, the knees loose and floppy. At 18 miles, 2350 feet, the trail at last touches Three Fools Creek and a possible camp; stop for an orgy of drinking and foot-soaking, and an understanding of why this trip is not recommended to begin at Ross Lake.

Hopes of an easy downhill water-grade hike are quickly dashed by a 1000-foot climb. The trail then goes down, goes up, and down and up, and finally on a forest bench to Lightning Creek at 23 miles, 1920 feet. Just before the crossing is a junction with the trail north to Nightmare Camp and Hozomeen (Hike 35). Just beyond the ford is Deer Lick Cabin (locked) and a campsite.

Again the trail climbs 1000 feet and goes down and up, high on the side of the Lightning Creek gorge, coming at last to a superb overlook of Ross Lake (reservoir), a thousand feet below. The conclusion is a switchbacking descent to the shore and Lightning Creek Camp, 1600 feet, 27 miles from Castle Pass.

Grouse

78 CADY PASS

Round trip 11 miles
Hiking time 6 hours
High point 6243 feet
Elevation gain 2400 feet

Hikable July through October
One day or backpack
USGS Slate Peak, Azurite Peak

Rock-and-ice giants of the North Cascades surround this grass-and-flower viewpoint. The trail is part of the fun—a narrow-gauge road (what is *that,* you ask?) built and used in the 1920s and 1930s by miners who hauled ore from their holes in the ground out over Harts Pass, whose tortuous road even today impresses the ordinary family-van driver as too darn narrow-gauge. The trail is also the aggravation, because mining claims keep the area excluded from wilderness or park protection—and now has been handed over by the Forest Service to the motorcycles. But this, too, will pass, if we keep the faith and keep writing those letters to our Congressmen.

Drive to Harts Pass (Hike 74) and continue down from the crest 5.2 rough miles towards Chancellor. At the second crossing of Slate Creek find Cady Pass trail No. 475, elevation 3550 feet.

The trail starts on abandoned road of 1950s-or-so vintage, not narrow gauge, gaining less than 100 feet in a scant 1½ miles to a steel bridge over South Fork Slate Creek. Here begins the narrow-gauge road of old. To answer your question, regular trucks were cut down to three-quarters scale, requiring a far narrower slice into the sides of the mountains, very handy for dirty miners.

The road-trail takes an easy grade up through grand forest. At one point it crosses a steep shale slope; if the tread has slid out, turn back. At about 3½ miles pass the foundations of a cabin; shortly beyond, note puncheon across a marshy area. The trail now leaves forest. Views expand. At Cady Pass, 5 miles, 6000 feet, they explode.

Go right from the pass on a faint path ½ mile along the ridge to a 6243-foot high point, one of the world's great places for looking around. To the west is Majestic Mountain, its 5-mile-long ridge rising high from depths

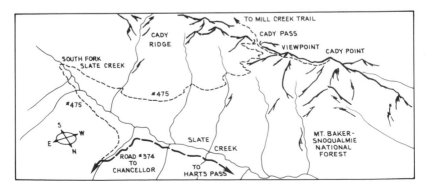

Mount Ballard from Cady Pass

of Mill Creek. Directly south on the same ridge as Cady Pass is 8300-foot Mt. Ballard. To the north is 8928-foot Jack Mountain, "King of the Skagit," and on the horizon west is the massive Neve Glacier on 8347-foot Snowfield Peak.

For views even better, drop about 150 feet, then climb to Cady Point, 6582 feet, site of a former lookout. Added, here, is a look down to the gorge of Canyon Creek. The sidetrip adds 1 mile to the round trip and 450 feet of elevation, going and coming.

79 CASCADE LOOP TRAIL— MONUMENT 83

Loop trip 34 miles
Allow 2–3 days
High point 6550 feet
Elevation gain 4900 feet

Hikable late June through
  October
USGS Frosty Creek and Castle
  Peak

When built in the 1920s the fire lookout at Monument 83 probably was the most remote in the Cascades. It still is if approached from the United States, via Slate Peak, West Fork Pasayten River, the pass near Deadwood Lake, and the Boundary Trail—a wilderness walk of nearly 30 miles that is well worth the doing, especially if part of a loop that returns down the Pacific Crest Trail. However, since construction of Highway 3

Old and new lookout buildings at Monument 83

across Manning Provincial Park in Canada, Monument 83 is only 10 miles from a road and lies on the very popular Cascade Loop Trail, featuring miles of splendid forest, climaxes of alpine meadows, and the thrill of (technically illegal) international travel.

Drive Highway 3 from Hope, British Columbia, across Allison Pass to Manning Provincial Park administration office, lodge, and visitors center ("Nature House"), where U.S. Forest Service wilderness permits (no longer needed) used to be available for camping in the Pasayten Wilderness. Park here, at the end of the loop hike, in order to have your car waiting, or drive 1.8 miles farther to the Monument 83 parking lot on the right side of the road, elevation 3700 feet.

The "trail" to Monument 83 is a rough, seldom-used service road, closed to public vehicles. In ¼ mile the way crosses the Similkameen River, then ascends gradually in forest along Chuwanten Creek and Monument Creek. At about 9 miles pass a sidetrail signed "Cathedral Lakes" and continue on the service road to the flowery little meadow of Monument 83, 10 miles, 6500 feet.

In the 1920s the U.S. Forest Service built the small log cabin on the highest point, which happens to lie in Canada. In 1953 the tower, tall enough to see over the foreign hill, was erected in America. The grave marker memorializes a pack mule that broke its leg and had to be shot.

From the lookout the now-true trail goes ¾ mile to join Boundary Trail No. 33, which descends 4½ miles along Chuchuwanteen (the American spelling of "Chuwanten") Creek to a campsite at the Frosty Creek crossing and a junction with trail No. 453, 4500 feet, 15 miles from Highway 3. Go right, upstream on Frosty Creek, to a camp ¼ mile past tiny Frosty Lake. The trail steepens and switchbacks to meadows of 6550-foot Frosty Pass, 21 miles, then drops 1 very steep mile to Castle Pass, 5451 feet, and a junction with the Pacific Crest Trail. Head north, passing water and a campsite in ½ mile. The Crest Trail descends gently above Route Creek, then Castle Creek, 3 miles to the border at Monument 78, then 7½ miles more along Castle Creek to Manning Park Headquarters.

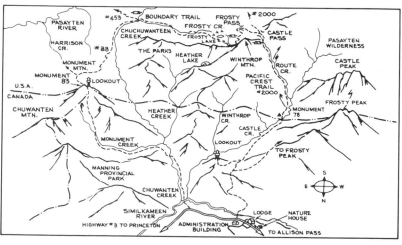

80 COPPER GLANCE LAKE

Round trip 6 miles
Hiking time 6 hours
High point 6400 feet
Elevation gain 2600 feet in, 300
feet out

Hikable June through October
One day or backpack
USGS Mazama

Beneath the cliffs of Isabella Ridge and 8204-foot Sherman Peak, ringed by fields of boulders and clumps of larch trees, sits Copper Glance Lake, a drop of snowmelt that by itself might scarcely be considered worth the walk. But, the walk is short. This is not to say it's *quick*. The trail gains 2500 feet in 3 miles. Some stretches are quite flat. All the worse—as any student of mountain mathematics understands, when a route that climbs this high is not very steep, a bit farther on it's going to have to be extremely steep to make up the difference. The spectacular scenery is worth the sweat. So are the meadows.

Drive the North Cascades Scenic Highway 20 to just west of Winthrop and then turn north on West Chewack River road, which in 6.5 miles becomes road No. 51. At 9 miles from the North Cascades Highway turn left on Eightmile Creek road No. 5130, signed "Billy Goat." In another 12.3 miles (the first 5 paved) find a gated jeep trail and Copper Glance trail No. 519 on the left side of the road and a small parking area on the right, elevation 3800 feet.

The trail starts on a steep mining road (gated) suitable only for jeeps. At about 1 mile, just after the second switchback, note remains of a log cabin. At 1½ miles is a mine shaft, 5200 feet, and the end of the mining road. True trail climbs on, at about 2 miles entering large, lush meadows dotted in season with lupine, aster, paintbrush, columbine, and valerian. The way returns to the woods, at 2¾ miles passing a small pond. That flatness has to be made up, and it is, by a supersteep ascent of a rockslide, topping out at 6400 feet. To loosen up the knees, the way descends 300 feet to the shore of the lake, 6100 feet.

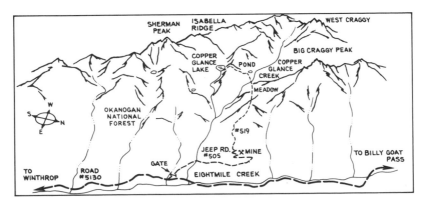

Copper Glance trail

81 PARSON SMITH TREE— HIDDEN LAKES

Round trip to Big Hidden Lake 35 miles
Allow 3 days
High point 5800 feet
Elevation gain 2400 feet in, 2700 feet out

Hikable late June through September
USGS Billy Goat Mountain, Lost Peak, Ashnola Mountain, and Tatoosh Buttes

> *I've roamed in many foreign parts my boys*
> *And many lands have seen.*
> *But Columbia is my idol yet*
> *Of all lands she is queen.*
>
> Parson Smith June 8, 1886

From the middle of the 19th century miners passed through the Pasayten on their way to Canadian gold fields. A few stopped to poke around. After all this time there is virtually no evidence of their passage except for Allen L. Smith, known as Parson Smith, prospector, sometimes trapper, artist, and poet, who on a return trip from Canada camped for a few days on the Pasayten River. There, on a pine tree just 12 feet from the U.S.–Canadian border, he carved the above poem.

Parson Smith's poem was first seen in 1903 when men from the International Boundary survey crew cleared a 10-foot swath on each side of the boundary line. The men noted the work of art but soon forgot it. It was rediscovered in 1913 by Rangers Frank Burge and George Wright. The tree was next seen in 1926 by Ranger Bill Lester. In 1965 the tree was dead and a shelter was built over the stump. In 1971 the stump was placed on the National Register of Historic Places. However, the shelter wasn't saving the wood from rot and the last straw was when a bear chewed up the stump. In 1980 this stump was moved to Early Winters Visitor Center and put in an airtight display case.

Today's hikers can see for themselves the pioneering route taken by Parson Smith. Drive from Winthrop 9 miles on Chewack River road (which becomes road No. 31), then 15 miles on Eightmile Creek road No. 5130 (Hike 80) to the end. The last mile, past Billy Goat Corral, leads to the hikers' parking area, elevation 4800 feet.

The trail follows a mine road about 100 feet; keep right. In ¼ mile, at Billy Goat Pass junction, keep left on Hidden Lakes trail No. 477. At 1¼ miles is a good view of Eightmile Pass and the steep gully Parson Smith may have descended. At 1½ miles cross the 5400-foot pass and drop to a campsite and bridge over Drake Creek, 4 miles from the road, 4600 feet. This is the last campsite with reliable water for the next 6 miles.

From Drake Creek climb 1200 feet in one long switchback to Lucky

Parson Smith Tree in Early Winters Visitor Center

Cougar Lake

Pass, 5800 feet, 6 miles from the road. At 8 miles pass Hoot Owl Camp (doubtful water supply) and at 10 miles reach a campground at the crossing of Diamond Creek, 4200 feet, lowest point of the trip.

Beyond Diamond Creek the trail climbs 300 feet, with ups and downs to dodge cliffs. Pass Deception Creek (underground most of the summer). At about 13 miles the trail finally comes close to Lost River and enters a fine old-growth forest that was spared by the great fire around 1920. At 14 miles, 4300 feet, is lovely Cougar Lake and campsites. At 15½ miles is a usually dried-up, unnamed lake, and at 16 miles the First Hidden Lake. Beyond are two Forest Service patrol cabins and separate campsites for horses and hikers. Next is Middle Hidden Lake, a slight rise, and the crossing-over to Pasayten drainage. The trail soon reaches 1½ - mile-long Big Hidden Lake, 4300 feet, 17½ miles from the road.

Most hikers are content to turn around here, but in 1½ miles, at the far end of Big Hidden Lake, wonders are to be seen: a large shelter, a buggy seat (not from bugs, but as in horse-and-buggy), and a rusted plow. A final 7½ miles lead to the Canadian border, where Parson Smith carved his tree; however, don't look for it there; go instead to the Early Winters Visitor Center.

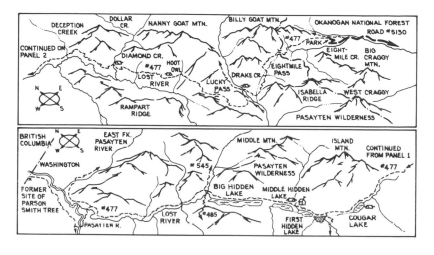

Gully used by early travelers over Eightmile Pass

82 BILLY GOAT PASS— BURCH MOUNTAIN

Round trip 10 miles
Hiking time 5 hours
High point 7782 feet
Elevation gain 3000 feet

Hikable late June through
October
One day
USGS Billy Goat Mountain

Hike to the edge of the Pasayten Wilderness, climb toward an old lookout site, and see miles and miles of broad valleys and open ridges. Carry plenty of water and start early before the sun gets hot. This is big-scale country, often with long stretches between points of scenic interest. For hikers, therefore, early summer is the best season, when flowers and snowfields add variety.

Big Craggy Peak from Burch Mountain trail

Drive to the parking area at the end of Eightmile Creek road (Hike 80), elevation 4800 feet.

Walk the mining road up Eightmile Creek, staying right at the first junction (unmarked). In about ¼ mile the trail splits. The left goes to Eightmile Pass (Hike 81); go right and zigzag steeply up 1800 feet in 3 miles 2½ miles through open forest to Billy Goat Pass, 6600 feet, on the border of Pasayten Wilderness.

Hike a few hundred feet over the pass and find Burch Mountain trail No. 516 angling upward on the east (right-hand) side. This well-constructed trail was once used by horses to supply a lookout on top of Burch Mountain. At first the tread is lost in meadows but as the hillside steepens the trail becomes distinct and, except for an occasional tree growing in the path, following it is no problem. The ascent is abrupt, quickly emerging to views southeast to Isabella Ridge and beyond to a horizon of 8000-foot peaks, the most dramatic being Big Craggy. Gaining some 600 feet in ¾ mile, the trail nearly reaches the ridge top, then con tours around a high, rocky knoll to a broad saddle at 7200 feet. From there it switchbacks up to the 7782-foot summit of Burch Mountain, 5 miles from the road-end. The lookout cabin has been gone many years but the views are as good as ever.

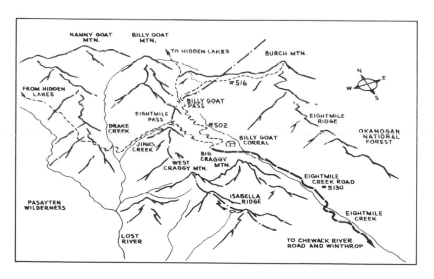

83 DOLLAR WATCH MOUNTAIN

Round trip 28 miles
Allow 3–4 days
High point 7679 feet
Elevation gain 5100 feet in, 1800 feet out

Hikable mid-July through mid-September
USGS Billy Goat Mountain, Lost Peak, Ashnola Mountain

This is a country for the fanciful. There are fanciful names, fanciful views, and trails to take you anywhere you fancy to go. Dollar Watch Mountain sits smack in the middle, ideal as a destination in itself or as a sidetrip on a many-day loop. Campsites are plentiful; some even have water all summer.

Drive to the end of Eightmile Creek road (Hike 80) and the hikers' parking area, elevation 4800 feet.

Hike from the end of Eightmile Creek road 2½ miles to Billy Goat pass, 6600 feet (Hike 82).

Pause to enjoy the long view out to rolling hills of the Methow Valley, then cross over. In a hundred feet pass the Burch Mountain trail (Hike 82) and plunge on down to Drake Creek, 5500 feet. Good camps here—with water, yet. At 5 miles cross Two Bit Creek and join the Drake Creek trail. The united way ascends an old burn to the broad gap (scoured out by the continental glacier) of Three Fools Pass, 6000 feet, and casually drops through woods and meadow towards Diamond Creek. At 6½ miles, about ½ mile below the pass, pass a well-used campsite, and at 7 miles, Diamond Point trail No. 514. Stay left on trail No. 502, cross the creek, 5500 feet, and begin a long sidehill, keeping nearly constant elevation into the valley of Larch Creek.

At 8½ miles turn left on trail No. 451A (perhaps unsigned) and in the next ½ mile drop to Larch Creek, 5500 feet. In a hundred yards the trail splits again, the right fork returning to Larch Creek trail, the left climbing to Dollar Watch.

The Dollar Watch trail climbs steadily with occasional views south to Three Fools Pass and Nanny Goat Mountain. At 2 miles above Larch Creek it passes through the upper basin of Tony Creek, the last reliable water supply before Dollar Watch Pass and Mountain. At 3 miles above

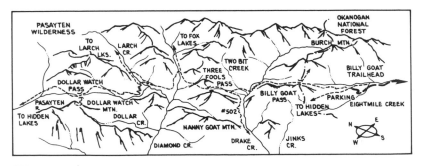

Snowstorm near summit of Dollar Watch Mountain

Larch Creek, 12 miles from the road, the faint tread of trail No. 451 branches right (east), crossing Two Point Mountain to reach Larch Pass, the first of several loop possibilities. Shortly beyond here the main trail crosses Dollar Watch Pass, 6950 feet, and drops to a campsite bench, 6870 feet, and a junction with East Fork Pasayten River trail No. 451.

The old lookout trail up Dollar Watch is lost in the bench meadows, so contour the upper slopes, find tread again, and climb to a saddle at 7063 feet. The trail branches; keep right, switchbacking to the old lookout site atop Dollar Watch Mountain, 7679 feet, 14 miles from the road. Presumably the watch was an Ingersoll pocket turnip. (Mickey Mouse watches came later.)

Black Lake

84 BLACK LAKE

Round trip 8½ miles
Hiking time 4 hours
High point 3982 feet
Elevation gain 800 feet

Hikable mid-May through
October
One day or backpack
USGS Mount Barney

A mile long, surrounded by forested peaks 7000 feet high, and a quick and easy walk from the road, Black Lake may be the most popular spot in the whole Pasayten Wilderness.

Drive from Winthrop 20.7 miles on the Chewack River road (Hike 80). Turn left on Lakes Creek road No. (5160)100 for 2.4 miles to the road-end and trail No. 500, elevation 3162 feet.

With only minor ups and downs, the trail follows close by Lake Creek in delightful forest; come in early August to feast your way on blueberries and raspberries, usually ripe by then. At about 1½ miles note a boulder, 10 by 20 feet, that rumbled down the ridge in the winter of 1984–85, crashed and smashed through the trees, and came to rest wedged between four trees just a few feet from the trail.

Having entered the Pasayten Wilderness along the way, at a little over 2 miles the trail reaches the shore of Black Lake, 3982 feet, 4¼ miles. Both ends of the lake have campsites; those at the far end may be horsier.

The crowds stop at the lake. For solitude continue a mile along the shore path, 7 more miles to tiny Fawn Lake, and then just keep on tramping, deeper into the heart of wildness.

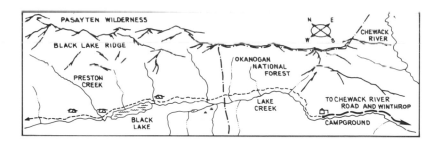

85 ANDREWS CREEK— CATHEDRAL LAKES

Round trip 42 miles
Allow 5–7 days
High point 7400 feet
Elevation gain 4800 feet in, 400
feet out

Hikable July through September
USGS Remmel Mountain, Mount
Barney, and Coleman Peak

The most-photographed scene in the eastern Pasayten Wilderness is Upper Cathedral Lake, sitting in a rock bowl amid ice-polished slabs, beneath the leaping cliffs of 8601-foot Cathedral Peak and 8358-foot Amphitheater Mountain. Cameras infest the place in fall, when the larch trees are bright gold, but also in summer, carried on hands and knees over the miles of lush herbaceous meadows and stony tundra, which demand the close-up lens. For all the beauty and the fame, though, crowds are thin, held down by 21 miles of trail.

Drive from Winthrop 23 miles on the Chewack River road (Hike 80) to Andrews Creek trail No. 504, elevation 3050 feet.

The trail has a fit of steepness at the start but after crossing Little Andrews Creek and a little divide settles down, at about ½ mile dropping a bit into Andrews Creek valley. Alternating between long valley-bottom flats and short, abrupt steps, it proceeds patiently toward its remote destination. At about 1 mile begins the 2-mile swath of a 1984 forest fire. At 3⅓ miles, near Blizzard Creek, pass two small buildings and the cable car of a stream-gauging station. At about 4 miles the path divides into two one-way lanes. Keep left, traversing a steep hillside too narrow to pass horses. The return route, a wide horse trail, gains 200 feet. (This is another example of forgetting hikers—the lower trail could be signed "hikers only" and save them a wearisome 200-foot ascent.)

At 5½ miles pass the Meadow Lake trail. At about 8 miles begins an earnest climb to Andrews Pass, 6700 feet, 13 miles from the road. On one side rises the west face of Remmel Mountain, on the other the rounded dome of Andrews Peak.

The way now loses 400 feet into Spanish Creek valley, at 15 miles passing the Spanish Creek trail. The ever-expanding meadows submerge memories of the long, sweaty, and usually fly-bitten miles. Choose a spot for a basecamp near the junction with the Boundary Trail, close by the tread or off in a secluded nook. But *do* camp *here*—the sites at Cathedral Lakes are few and small and probably full and those at Remmel Lake are very horsey.

Boundary trail No. 523 goes right, passing Chewack trail No. 510, to Upper Cathedral Lake, 7400 feet, 21 miles from the road. You definitely will want to walk the roller-skate-smooth slabs and examine the gouges made by the glaciers; this area has experienced both local alpine glaciation, from such cirques as that of the Cathedral Lakes, and continental glaciation from accumulation centers in Canada, which sent out ice sheets that rode over and rounded the tops of all the peaks in the eastern Pasayten except a very few, including Cathedral.

You also may wish to drop on a sidetrail to Lower Cathedral Lake. Nor should you forget that the Boundary Trail goes west, ascending to just under the summit of Bald Mountain; spend a night on top and see who comes to the dance. A very large proportion of the Cascades terrain that satisfies the technical definition of "tundra" is located hereabouts; wander it this way and that, to the summit ridge of Amphitheater, should it please you. Sit amid the high-alpine blossoms and the lichen-covered stones and gaze to the Arctic Ocean.

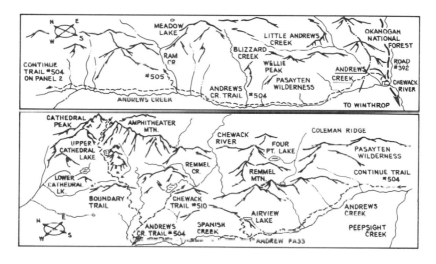

Cathedral Lake

Remmel Mountain from Remmel Lake

CHEWACK RIVER
Pasayten Wilderness

CHEWACK RIVER—
REMMEL LAKE

Round trip 34 miles
Allow 3–5 days
High point 6871 feet
Elevation gain 3400 feet

Hikable July through September
USGS Remmel Mountain,
   Coleman Peak, and Bauerman
Ridge

Much of what has been said about Cathedral Lakes (Hike 85) also can be said about Remmel Lake—and indeed, they are near enough together

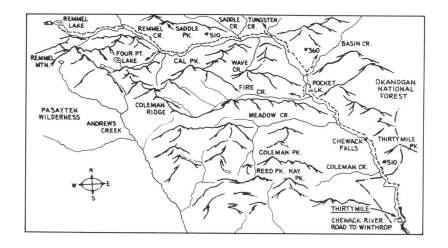

that visiting back and forth is easy and quick. There are meadows around the shore, covered in season with blue lupine and deep red paintbrush and yellow "sunflowers." There are higher and drier meadows—true tundra, as in the Arctic, spongy and wet early in the season, buckled into small ridges and mounds by frost heaves, and peppered with innumerable holes of Columbian ground squirrels—"rockchucks" which behave in a most marmotlike manner, diving into their homes to escape the ever-patroling raptors, as well as the fun-loving humans who carry .22 pistols for the amiable all-seasons sport of "plinking."

Drive from Winthrop 30 miles on the Chewack River road (Hike 80) to its end at Thirtymile Camp and the start of Chewack River trail No. 510, elevation 3500 feet.

Heavily stomped and tramped by horses and hikers, the trail starts wide and dusty and pretty much stays that way, except when it's wide and muddy. In 1 mile it enters the Pasayten Wilderness. Just 300 feet are gained in the scant 3 miles to Chewack Falls. The way passes swampy Pocket Lake to the junction with the Fire Creek Coleman Ridge trail (Hike 87) at about 5 miles, and at 8 miles Tungsten Creek trail, having gained thus far only 1100 feet. At 12 miles is the junction with Four Point Lake—Coleman Ridge trail (Hike 87). The tread now grows tired, worn, and rocky but the angle inclines upward only a little as forest thins to parkland. The rugged north face of Remmel Mountain appears and the path flattens to the shore of Remmel Lake, 6871 feet, 14 miles from the road.

If there were a market for horse apples, this would be a good field to harvest. The lake is ringed with campsites but unless one has grown up in a barnyard and *likes* that smell, finding a spot to eat supper is a problem. One would think that the Forest Service would keep horses at least 500 feet from camps and lakeshores or designate some of the campsites for hikers. For clean camps continue above the lake to a small creek. But watch out for sheep, too. They also have the right-of-way over hikers.

87 FOUR POINT LAKE— COLEMAN RIDGE LOOP

Loop trip 41 miles
Allow 3–5 days
High point 7300 feet
Elevation gain 4000 feet

Hikable late June through
September
USGS Remmel Mountain,
Bauerman Ridge, and Coleman
Peak

If Four Point Lake alone is the goal—as it may well be, rimmed as it is with white granite, pines and larch, and a silver forest, with views to the cliffs of 8685-foot Remmel Peak—the easiest approach is to hike the Chewack River trail (Hike 86) 12 miles and turn left for 3 miles on the Four Point Lake trail. However, long and rugged though the loop is, there are compensations.

Drive from Winthrop 30 miles on the Chewack River road (Hike 80) to its end at Thirtymile Camp and the start of Chewack River trail No. 510, elevation 3500 feet.

Hike the Chewack River trail (Hike 86) 5¼ miles and turn left on the Fire Creek-Coleman Ridge trail. Ford the river (no cinch in early summer), 4782 feet, and strike off up the steep trail, torn to shreds by cows (they graze here in alternate years), gain 800 feet in switchbacks, then moderating. The way traverses a succession of meadows where tread is lost in a maze of cow tracks and pies (when thoroughly dry, these latter make as satisfactory a fire as buffalo chips). In one of the cow-mushed meadow-marshes, watch for a hiking boot half-buried in muck; wonder what became of the hiker?

At about 6 miles from the Chewack River the trail tops the divide, 6800 feet, between Fire Creek and Andrews Creek and proceeds steeply up the meadows of Coleman Ridge to 7200 feet. When the tread vanishes,

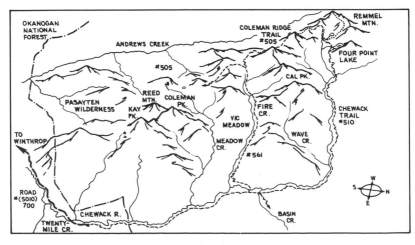

Remmel Mountain from trail on Coleman Ridge

watch for cairns. At the ridge-end the trail plummets some 300 feet, then climbs more meadows to a saddle between Andrews Creek and Four Point Creek. Here is a view to Four Point Lake. An ascent to a 7300-foot high point is followed by a descent over a rockslide of gleaming white granite. At 11 miles from the Chewack River (16 miles from the road) a little detour leads to the shore of Four Point Lake, 6830 feet.

A horse trail once continued to the top of 8685-foot Remmel Mountain to service the fire lookout located there from 1932 to 1956. The trail was abandoned and expunged from government maps, but hikers report the tread survives the official "disappearing." From the spur to Four Point Lake go back about ¼ mile, follow a stream up to a small tarn, and scout on the hillside for evidence of human and equine presence.

To complete the loop, descend steeply 3 miles (the sign says 2) from the lake to a ford of the Chewack River, an easy step when the water is low, and proceed down and out 12 miles to the car.

88 HONEYMOON CREEK— NORTH TWENTYMILE PEAK

Round trip 13 miles
Hiking time 7 hours
High point 7464 feet
Elevation gain 4200 feet

Hikable June through October
One day or backpack
USGS Doe Mountain and
**   Coleman Peak**

Behold an infinity of forested ridges extending from Silver Star Mountain in the west to Canada north, Tiffany Mountain east, and beyond the Methow Valley south. In all the wild scene only a single road can be seen,

Historic lookout built in late 1920s on North Twentymile Peak

along the Chewack River a vertical mile below. Ah, but the hand of man, if hidden, is everywhere busy, sawing and chopping. To be sure, no clear-cuts give him away because the logging is selective, meaning he is selecting the beautiful, big, old Ponderosa pine and Douglas fir, leaving the small trees, which never will be allowed to grow old, big, and beautiful unless placed in protected wilderness.

Drive the North Cascades Scenic Highway 20 to just west of Winthrop and turn north on West Chewack River road, which in 6.5 miles becomes road No. 51. At 17.6 miles from the North Cascades Highway turn right .6 mile on road No. 5010, then left 2 miles on road No. (5010)700 to the trailhead, elevation 3200 feet. Fill the canteens before starting, for this is the *eastern* North Cascades where the sun shines bright all day, except during thunderstorms.

Trail No. 560 starts on an abandoned logging road that yields to true trail with good tread, gaining 500–800 feet a mile. At 2 miles is the first and last water, at a campsite beside Honeymoon Creek. At about 5 miles the way attains the ridge crest and views that grow steadily in the last 1½ miles to the summit, 7464 feet.

An abandoned trail goes east 10 miles to Thirtymile Meadows and road No. 39. If the proposed Twentymile–Thirtymile Wilderness is not established (as it was *not* by the 1984 Washington Wilderness Act), this trail likely will be reopened—for motorcycles. Barring that catastrophe, the first mile along the ridge from the summit is a marvelous meadow stroll. One would love to camp here, if one could find (or carry) water. But one would not love to be here when lightning bolts are zapping prominently upright organisms.

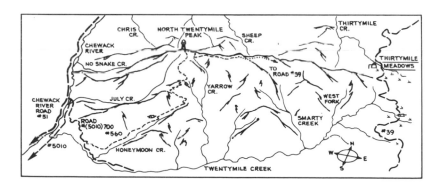

89 SMARTY CREEK— NORTH TWENTYMILE PEAK

Round trip 17 miles
Hiking time 9 hours
High point 7437 feet
Elevation gain 1600 feet in, 300
  feet out

Hikable June through October
One day or backpack
USGS Tiffany Mountain, Coleman
  Peak, Horseshoe Basin

Miles of meadows, then miles of ridge-walking, then the historic fire-lookout cabin atop North Twentymile Peak, with from-here-to-forever views of forests and valleys and mountains. The flowers, the ridge vistas, the modest elevation gain, and the many good camps make this route much richer in rewards than via Honeymoon Creek (Hike 88). However, the trail is seldom used, seldom maintained, and no manufacturer's miracle boots will keep the feet dry through the endless succession of bogs. (Bog-lovers don't care. They love to watch the butterwort suck the juices from dead flies.)

Drive from Winthrop on either the East or West Chewack River road (see Hikes 60 and 88) about 7 miles. Just a few feet east of the Chewack River bridge where the two roads join, turn north on road No. 37. In 1.2 miles keep right on road No. 37 as it climbs along Boulder Creek. At 11.5 miles go left on road No. 39. The road becomes rougher and steeper as it climbs over a 6500-foot saddle in Freezeout Ridge and then drops and again climbs to a 6900-foot saddle near Tiffany Springs Campground and the end of gravel road. The last 1.5 miles are rough, steep, and not maintained for passenger cars, so if that is what is being driven, go very slowly. At 8.7 miles from the junction of roads Nos. 37 and 39, cross South Fork Twentymile Creek and find trail No. 371, elevation 5900 feet.

The trail follows the creek downstream, mostly in glorious meadows (and bogs), the tread almost impossible to find but the route obvious. At

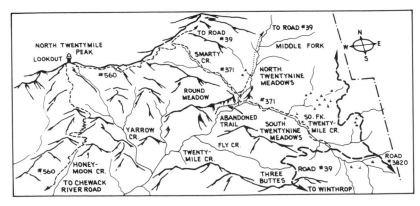

about 2 miles the meadows end as the valley narrows to a V. Finding the trail, and staying on it, become very important here. At 2½ miles is a junction and an ancient trail sign. Go right, up North Fork Twentymile Creek, a scant ½ mile. Cross the creek and climb steeply to another junction and sign. Go left, downstream a bit, then up along Smarty Creek, skirting one final meadow. An earnest climb leads to the ridge top and at 5 miles another junction. Go left on trail No. 560, up and down the crest in picture-window views steadily enlarging. The crest rises at last above timberline and the views climax atop North Twentymile Peak, 7437 feet, 8½ miles from the road.

The lookout cabin was built in 1923 and may be the state's last surviving example of the cupola design. Until quite recently it was staffed every summer.

Headwaters of North Twentymile Creek

Tiffany Mountain from Tiffany Meadows

CHEWACK RIVER
Unprotected area

90   TIFFANY MOUNTAIN

**Round trip from Freezeout Pass
to the summit 6 miles**
Hiking time 4 hours
High point 8242 feet
Elevation gain 1700 feet
Hikable July through September

One day
USGS Tiffany Mountain

**One-way trip via Tiffany Lake 8
miles**
Hiking time 5 hours

A superb ridge walk to an 8242-foot summit with views west to distant peaks of the North Cascades, north into the Pasayten Wilderness, and east to farmlands of the Okanogan. The hike can be done as a round trip or—by use of two cars or a non-hiking assistant to move the car—as a one-way trip to either of two alternate trailheads.

Drive north from Winthrop on the paved East Chewack River road. At 7.5 miles, just before the paved road crosses the Chewack River, turn right on road No. 37. In less than 2 miles turn right again, still on road No. 37, which now follows Boulder Creek. In 11.5 miles go left on road No. 39 and continue 3 miles on very poor road to Freezeout Pass and the trailhead, elevation 6500 feet.

(To place a car at the first of the alternate trailheads, drive 4 more miles to Tiffany Lake trail, 6240 feet. For the second, drive beyond the lake trail 5 miles on road No. 39 to a junction, turn right 1 mile on road No. 3820 to Lone Frank Pass, and go another 6 miles to the trailhead, 4990 feet, signed "Tiffany Lake trail." If you reach Salmon Meadows you've driven about 1 mile too far.)

From Freezeout Pass the trail climbs steadily 1½ miles through trees, then 1 mile above timberline, and begins a contour around the east side of the peak. Be sure to make the ½-mile (each way) sidetrip up grassy slopes to the unlimited views from the top of Tiffany Mountain, once the site of a fire lookout.

For the one-way trips, return to the trail and continue onward, descending through Whistler Pass to a 6800-foot junction, 3½ miles from Freezeout Pass, with the Tiffany Lake trail. Either go 4 miles to the road via 6480-foot Tiffany Lake or follow the open ridge above the North Fork Salmon Creek 2½ miles before dropping into trees and down to the road.

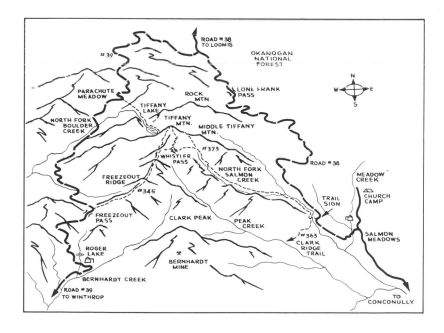

91 BERNHARDT TRAIL

Round trip to North Summit 6 miles
Hiking time 4 hours
High point 7200 feet
Elevation gain 1800 feet

Hikable July through September
One day
USGS Tiffany Mountain

Sometimes steep and sometimes very steep, the trail named for Mr. (or Ms.) Bernhardt (we don't know who he or she was, or is) ascends through forest to fields of windswept or sunstruck or rain-flattened grass on the slopes of Clark Peak. At its junction with the North Summit trail a hiker has three options: climb Clark Peak; climb Tiffany Mountain; or take off on an 11-mile loop.

Drive from Winthrop on the East Chewack River road 7.5 miles and just before the Chewack River bridge go right on road No. 37, following the river a short way, then climbing into Boulder Creek valley. In another 12.7 miles (sign says, "Winthrop 19 miles") go left on road No. 39 for 1.2 miles and find Bernhardt trail No. 367, elevation 5700 feet.

In a scant ½ mile the trail crosses Bernhardt Creek and then a tributary—twice. In about 1 mile it skirts a boggy meadow and around 1½ miles starts up, seldom bothering with switchbacks. At about 2¼ miles the path goes left of a sturdy log cabin with a leaky roof (attention, Bernhardt family) to an unmarked junction. The right dead-ends in ½ mile at some diggings, presumably Bernhardt's; go left, in the sometimes-steeply gear, taking care not to stray off on the many animal paths. At 3 miles, 7200 feet, are North Summit trail No. 369 and the options.

Option 1: Turn around and go home. But first, sidetrip left ¼ mile for a striking view of Freezeout Ridge and Tiffany Mountain.

Option 2: Pick your own way up open slopes to the top of Clark Peak, 7900 feet.

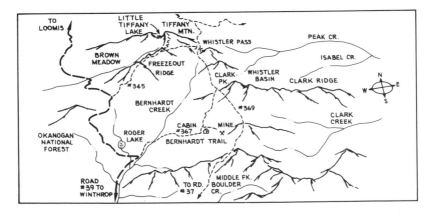

Old cabin with leaky roof on Bernhardt trail

Option 3: Go left, north, on the North Summit trail a very scant 2 miles to Whistler Pass, 7600 feet. Stay on the trail to the summit of Tiffany Mountain, 8242 feet. Descend Freezeout Ridge trail No. 345 to road No. 39 and walk it downhill 2 miles to the Bernhardt trailhead, for a loop total of 11 miles.

92 NORTH SUMMIT TRAIL

Round trip 11 miles
Hiking time 6 hours
High point 7500 feet
Elevation gain 2300 feet in, 250
  feet out

Hikable June through September
One day
USGS Tiffany Mountain (trail not
  shown)

The North Summit trail is an old stock driveway, which might not sound much like fun, but the cows and sheep haven't been around these

Tiffany Mountain from North Summit Trail

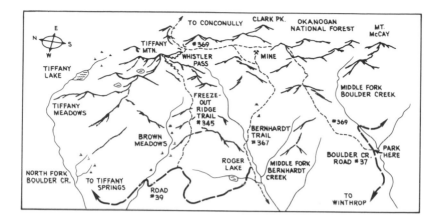

parts in years, ever since the cowboys and shepherds moved their enter-
prises to the lower country, where they were less likely to have their
animals frozen to death in an August blizzard. So, it's a long and
lonesome ridge of pines and meadows, the flora the more interesting because on sunny slopes there is sagebrush, and on wetter slopes, rock gardens of lupine, paintbrush, buckwheat, and stonecrop. The views, too, are
distinctive, combining long looks out to the rolling highlands of Eastern
Washington and long looks west to distant peaks of the North Cascades.
Closer up are the green meadows of Clark Peak and Tiffany Mountain.
Bring full canteens; there's no water.

By use of two cars, this trip can be combined with the Bernhardt trail
(Hike 91) or Tiffany Mountain (Hike 90).

Drive from Winthrop on the East Chewack River road 7.5 miles and
just before the Chewack River bridge go right on road No. 37, following
the river a short way, then climbing into Boulder Creek valley. In another 12.7 miles (sign says, "Winthrop 19 miles") go right another 2.5
miles to a gravel pit and North Summit trail No. 369, elevation 5400
feet.

The trail starts in the gravel pit, enters forest, and in ½ mile skirts the
top of a large sagebrush meadow, the route marked by large cairns. The
way returns to trees and at about 1¼ miles crosses another sagebrush
meadow, the cairns fewer and smaller; if you lose the route, contour and
climb, searching for cairns; find tread in the trees on the far side. Woods
and meadows alternating, the trail climbs to a 7500-foot saddle and
crosses the ridge to a great spot, 2½ miles from the road, to view the
world and call it a day.

From the viewspot the trail traverses the west side of the ridge, then
steeply drops 250 feet to a low point. It swings around the east slopes of
the next high point of the crest to the next low point at 3½ miles, and
here meets the Clark Ridge trail. The North Summit trail now contours
the west side of Clark Peak, passing the Bernhardt trail at 4½ miles and
at 5½ miles ending at Whistler Pass. At the pass is a four-way intersection offering a choice of climbing Tiffany Mountain, taking the Tiffany
Lake trail, descending the Freezeout Ridge trail, or turning around to go
back the way you came.

219

$\underline{93}$ HORSESHOE BASIN (PASAYTEN)

Round trip to Sunny Pass 9 miles
Hiking time 6 hours
High point 7200 feet
Elevation gain 1200 feet

Hikable late June through mid-
 October
One day or backpack
USGS Horseshoe Basin

At the northeast extremity of the Cascades is a tundra country so unlike the main range a visitor wonders if he hasn't somehow missed a turn and ended up in the Arctic. Meadows for miles and miles, rolling from broad basins to rounded summits of peaks above 8000 feet, with views south over forests to Tiffany Mountain, east to Chopaka Mountain and the Okanogan Highlands, north far into Canada, and west across the Pasayten Wilderness to glaciered, dream-hazy giants of the Cascade Crest.

Drive from Tonasket to Loomis and turn north. In 1.5 miles turn left at signs for Toats Coulee, cross the valley of Sinlahekin Creek, and start a long, steep climb up Toats Coulee on road No. 39. At 11 miles from Loomis is North Fork Campground and in another 5 miles a junction with a narrow, old, unnumbered road signed "Iron Gate." Turn right and drive 7 rough and steep miles to the road-end and trailhead, elevation 6000 feet, at the new Iron Gate Camp (no water) on the boundary of the Pasayten Wilderness.

The first ½ mile is downhill along the abandoned road to the old Iron Gate Camp (no water). The trail from here begins in small lodgepole pine (most of this region was burned off by a series of huge fires in the 1920s) on the old road to Tungsten Mine, which sold stock as recently as the early 1950s. The grade is nearly flat ½ mile to cool waters of a branch of Clutch Creek and then starts a moderate, steady ascent. At 3¼ miles the route opens out into patches of grass and flowers. After a brief steep bit, at 4 miles the way abruptly emerges from trees to the flowery, stream-bubbling nook of Sunny Basin and splendid Sunny Camp, 6900 feet.

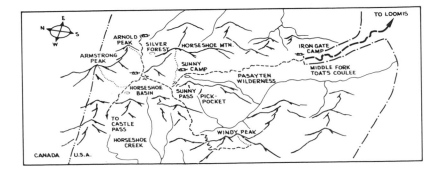

The trail climbs ½ mile to 7200-foot Sunny Pass—be prepared to gasp and rave. All around spreads the enormous meadowland of Horseshoe Basin, demanding days of exploration. From the pass the Tungsten road drops left and the "pure" trail goes right, contouring gentle slopes of Horseshoe Mountain to grand basecamps in and near the wide flat of Horseshoe Pass, 7100 feet, 5¾ miles, and then contouring more glory to tiny Louden Lake, 6¾ miles (this lake dries up in late summer), and then on and on as described in Hike 94.

The roamings are unlimited. All the summits are easy flower walks— 7620-foot Pick Peak, 8000-foot Horseshoe Mountain, and 8076-foot Arnold Peak. The ridge north from 8106-foot Armstrong Peak has the added interest of monuments to mark the United States—Canada boundary. A more ambitious sidetrip is south from Sunny Pass 6 miles on the down-and-up trail to 8334-foot Windy Peak, highest in the area and once the site of a fire lookout. Don't omit a short walk east through Horseshoe Pass to the immense silver forest at the head of Long Draw.

Louden Lake in Horseshoe Basin

Boundary Trail and Remmel Mountain near Cathedral Pass

SINLAHEKIN CREEK
Pasayten Wilderness

 # BOUNDARY TRAIL

One-way trip (main route) from
  Iron Gate via Castle Pass to
  Harts Pass 94 miles
Allow 10 days or more
High point 7600 feet
Elevation gain 15,000 feet
Hikable July through September

USGS Horseshoe Basin,
  Bauerman Ridge, Remmel
  Mountain, Ashnola Pass,
  Ashnola Mountain, Tatoosh
  Buttes, Frosty Creek, Castle
  Peak

As the golden eagle flies, it's 40 miles from the east edge of the Pasayten Wilderness to the Cascade Crest; as the backpacker walks it's twice that far, with some distance still remaining to reach civilization. Though the Pasayten country lacks the glaciers of more famous mountains west, and with few exceptions the peaks are rounded, unimpressive to a climber, there is a magnificent vastness of high ridges, snowfields, flower gardens, parklands, cold lakes, green forests, loud rivers. The weather is better and summer arrives earlier than in windward ranges. The trails are high much of the distance, often above 7000 feet, but are mostly snowfree in early July, an ideal time for the trip.

Length of the route precludes a detailed description in these pages. In any event the journey is for experienced wilderness travelers who have the routefinding skills needed to plan and find their own way. The notes below merely aim to stimulate the imagination.

Begin from the Iron Gate road-end (Hike 93) and walk to Horseshoe Basin and Louden Lake (6¾ miles). With ups and downs, always in highlands, the trail goes along Bauerman Ridge to Scheelite Pass (13¾ miles), the old buildings and garbage of Tungsten Mine (17¾ miles), and over Cathedral Pass to Cathedral Lakes (21¾ miles). The route this far makes a superb 4–7 day round trip from Iron Gate.

Continue west to Spanish Camp (26 miles) and the first descent to low elevation, at the Ashnola River (31½ miles). Climb high again, passing Sheep Mountain (34½ miles), Quartz Mountain (38 miles), and Bunker Hill (43¼ miles), then dropping to low forests of the Pasayten River (50½ miles).

Follow the Pasayten River upstream to the Harrison Creek trail No. 453 and cross a high ridge to Chuchuwanteen Creek (60 miles); at some time in the future this stretch may be rerouted via Soda Creek and Dead Lake. Ascend Frosty Creek past Frosty Lake to Frosty Pass (68 miles) and on to Castle Pass (66¾ miles). From here take the Pacific Crest Trail 27 miles south (Hike 100) to Harts Pass, ending a trip of some 94 miles.

(For a shorter alternate, hike up the Pasayten River to Three Forks and ascend the West Fork Pasayten to Harts Pass. Trails branch west from this valley route to reach the Cascade Crest at Woody Pass and Holman Pass.)

However, for the true and complete Boundary Trail, go west from Castle Pass on the Three Fools Trail (Hike 77), hike south to Ross Dam and cross Ross Lake to the Little Beaver, and traverse the North Cascades National Park via Whatcom and Hannegan Passes (Hike 12), concluding the epic at the Ruth Creek road.

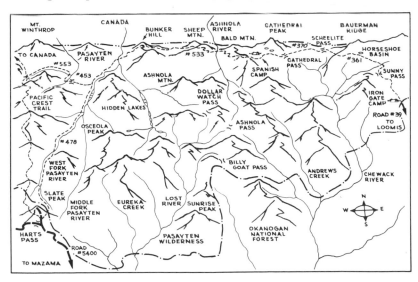

SINLAHEKIN CREEK
Unprotected area

95 CHOPAKA MOUNTAIN

Round trip 4 miles
Hiking time 4 hours
High point 7882 feet
Elevation gain 1700 feet

Hikable mid-May through June,
  before cows arrive
One day
USGS Loomis and Horseshoe
  Basin

Stand on the absolute easternmost peak of the North Cascades. Look down a startling 6700-foot scarp to green pastures and orchards around Palmer Lake and meanders of the Similkameen River. Look east to the Okanogan Highlands, north into Canada and the beginnings of other ranges, and south over rolling forests of Toats Coulee Creek to Tiffany Mountain. And also look west across the Pasayten Wilderness to haze-dimmed, snowy summits of the Chelan Crest and Washington Pass. Aside from the geographical distinction of "farthest east," the special feature of the hike is the opportunity to wander alpine meadows as early as May, when windward ranges are so deep in snow that the coming of flowers seems an impossible dream.

Drive from Tonasket to Loomis and turn north. In 1.5 miles turn left at signs for Chopaka Lake and Toats Coulee, cross the valley of Sinlahekin Creek, ignore a road that goes right and uphill to Chopaka Lake, and start a long, steep climb up Toats Coulee on road No. 39. At 10 miles from Loomis, turn right 8 miles on the Ninemile Creek road (at this and all subsequent junctions follow "Chopaka Mountain" signs) to Cold Spring Campground, 6000 feet. The road generally is snowfree by Memorial Day; before then the way may be blocked by lingering snowfields, but if so this merely adds a mile or two to the hike.

Drive ¼ mile above Cold Spring to the road-end parking lot and campground (no water), elevation 6200 feet, with views west to Horseshoe Basin country. Hike a jeep track through spindly trees ½ mile. At 6600 feet, where the ruts start a sidehill contour northeast, find the first logical meadow opening and leave the track, climbing an obvious way toward the heights. The ascent winds amid clumps of alpine trees on open ground that would be flower-glorious were it not devastated by cattle. However, a slope of frost-wedged boulders stops the hooves and marks

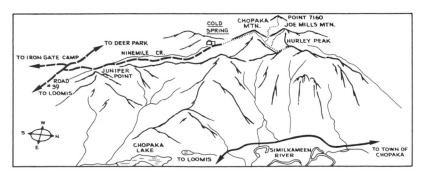

224

Chopaka Mountain

the upper end of mud wallows and cow pies; the meadows now become genuine, clean, and natural. Emerge onto a broad plateau and amble a few more feet to the 7882-foot summit.

If another couple of hours are available, even better views can be had from Hurley Peak, a mile away. Drop north down a superb heather-and-flower meadow to a 7300-foot saddle and climb a gentle ridge to the 7820-foot top.

96 GOLDEN STAIRWAY

Round trip 8 miles
Hiking time 5 hours
High point 6500 feet
Elevation gain 2100 feet

Hikable May through October
One day
USGS Tiffany Mountain

The fields of flowers are as pretty as flower fields anywhere, and the sweat flows as freely on the steeps of the trail. However, the views down to Conconully Reservoir and out over the rolling hills of north-central

Trail on Cathedral Driveway

Washington are unfamiliar to most residents of the state, the preponderance of whom live far to the west, many mountains away. But increasingly these outlanders are learning to appreciate and love the north-central country—to which this walk is a neat and easy introduction.

Drive from Conconully on county road No. 2017 around the west side of the reservoir and up Salmon Creek. Turn right on road No. 37 about 5 miles, go left on road No. 3700(400), and in another .7 mile go left again on road No. 3700(420). Proceed 2 more miles to its end and the start of trail No. 354, elevation 4400 feet. (Logging could change this beginning.)

The trail commences with a short drop and a crossing of West Fork Salmon Creek. It climbs a bit, paralleling an abandoned logging road, then follows the West Fork upstream. At ½ mile cross Jim Creek and at 1½ miles, West Fork again. At about 2 miles, having gained only 600 feet so far, the way steepens to a 15 to 20 percent grade and in the next 2 miles gains 1500 feet, an ideal rate of ascent (and descent) for a hiker. (Horses prefer 10 percent, the Forest Service says, but there are a lot more of us than them, so why are we discriminated against?)

At 3 miles forest yields to a steep meadow, a color riot in early July with red paintbrush, cream buckwheat, blue lupine and larkspur, and yellow arnica. At 4 miles the switchbacks top the ridge crest, 6400 feet, and intersect Cathedral (stock) Driveway trail No. 369. The trail straight ahead continues 2 miles, dropping 500 feet to Beaver Meadow. To the left the Cathedral Driveway climbs very steeply over a 6689-foot high point. The trail to the right is recommended, ambling an easy ⅓ mile to a 6500-foot knoll. Sit at ease, bring out the cucumbers and cherry tomatoes and flagon of kumquat juice and contemplate Conconully, nestled in the hills. If you lived in Conconully, these would be your home views. Not bad.

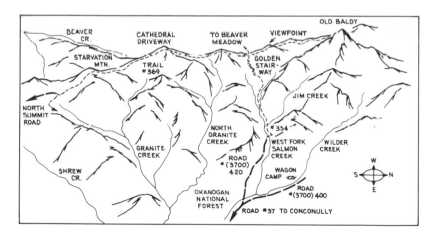

97 MOUNT BONAPARTE

Round trip 9 miles
Hiking time 6 hours
High point 7258 feet
Elevation gain 2752 feet

Hikable mid-June through
    October
One day
USGS Mt. Bonaparte

No, campers, we're not in the North Cascades here, but well to the east across the Okanogan Valley, in highlands that may be considered a suburb of the Selkirk Range. Two unique features of the mountain are the highest fire lookout in Eastern Washington and the original lookout building, constructed in 1914 of hand-hewn logs (see the ax marks) and now on the National Register of Historic Buildings.

Among the 20 miles of trail in the roadless area (proposed for wilderness status, but omitted from the 1984 Washington Wilderness Act, leaving the job still to be done) around Mt. Bonaparte are three routes to the top, each with its own attractions. The South Side trail, 5½ miles long, starts at 4400 feet on road No. (3300)100 and gives views of Bonaparte Lake. Antoine trail, 6 miles, *presently* starts on private property so it is not recommended. The Myers Creek trail described here is the shortest and starts highest, but the way is dry and no views until the summit.

Drive east from the north end of Tonasket on county road No. 9467, signed "Sitzmark Ski Area—Havillah." In 15.7 miles, just short of Havillah Church, turn right on a road signed "Lost Lake." Pavement ends in .9 mile; turn right on road No. 33. At 4.2 miles from the county road turn right on road No. (3300)300 (abbreviated on the sign to 300). Follow it 1.2 miles to the trailhead, elevation 4500 feet.

Mt. Bonaparte trail No. 306 starts on a logging road, crosses a creek, and climbs ¼ mile to a permanent roadblock (some cars drive this far). The trail itself is, or was, a road, now abandoned, through a replanted clearcut. Dodge several motorcycle trails; follow horse and foot prints straight ahead. At 1¼ miles is the end of logging and the start of virgin forest of lodgepole pine. The trail steepens to a junction at 2½ miles with the South Side trail. At 3¾ miles is a junction with the Antoine trail. Lodgepole pines yield to subalpine fir, which at 4½ miles yields to open meadows and all-around-the-compass views over forested hills to valley ranches. The summit of the Okanogan Highlands has been attained, 7258 feet.

Below the modern lookout tower is the 1914 lookout building, slightly bent out of shape by the weight of winter snow. The tower atop the cabin had to be removed years ago. In early days the lookout communicated by heliograph, an instrument that aimed a beam of sunlight and by means of a shutter transmitted Morse Code to a receiver as far away as 20–30 miles. On cloudy days and at night the lookout did not communicate— until telephone lines were installed in the 1930s. When the lines were broken by falling trees or limbs the lookout did not communicate—until the 1960s and the magic of radio.

Old (1914) and new lookout buildings on Mount Bonaparte

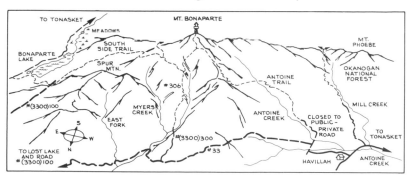

South Kettle Range from Columbia Mountain

KETTLE RANGE
Unprotected area

98   KETTLE CREST TRAIL—NORTH

**Round trip to Columbia Mountain
5½ miles
Hiking time 3 hours
High point 6782 feet
Elevation gain 1400 feet
Hikable mid-May through
   September
One day
USGS Sherman Peak**

**Round trip to Copper Butte 26
  miles
Allow 2 days
High point 7135 feet
Elevation gain 2900 feet in, 1200
  feet out
Hikable mid-June through
  October
USGS Sherman Peak, Copper
  Butte, Cook Mountain, and Mt.
  Leona**

Known the past century and more almost solely by local folk, in recent years the Kettle Range has begun building toward what will be, before long, wide fame. These are friendly mountains—no beetling crags, no glaciers, no roaring waterfall-torrents, and not much in the way of remoteness because the peaks lie in a narrow line with numerous access trails from all sides. However, the views offer miles and miles of rolling hills, the alternation of herbaceous (wet) meadows and sagebrush-steppe (dry) meadows, plus the mix of Ponderosa pine and aspen in the forests, have an enchantment of their own. That they were omitted from the 1984 Washington Wilderness Act stirred such a protest as never will die until the wrong is righted. Meanwhile, thanks to a sympathetic ranger who has used the excuse of possible environmental damage to the meadows, the whole Kettle Crest Trail is (legally) motorfree.

Columbia Mountain, where a lookout was built in 1914, has glorious views near and far, a great day from the car. The energetic can do more—continue 4 miles to the large meadows on Wapaloosie Mountain. Backpackers can proceed to the highest peak in the range, Copper Butte. As is true of any ridge-top trail, water is scarce after the snow melts; most backpackers therefore make entry via one of the valley trails, not so thirsty as the heights. Snow leaves earlier here than in the Cascades and usually is mostly gone by mid-May; hikers with ice axes sometimes can ramble in late April. However, snowpatches can linger in shady corners well into June.

From Republic on the west or Kettle Falls on the east drive Highway 20 to the summit of Sherman Pass and turn north to the trailhead parking area, elevation 5400 feet.

The trail, built for horses and thus commodious, is moderately steep the first mile of open forest. Granite knolls and buttresses smoothed or plucked by the continental glacier nourish brilliant rock gardens. The way moderates, contouring Columbia Mountain to a broad sagebrush meadow. Just beyond the 2-mile marker the sidetrail climbs a very steep ¾ mile to Columbia Mountain, 6782 feet, and the big views.

With moderate ups and down the main trail contours onward north. At a bit over 4 miles it drops 500 feet, then climbs through the vast meadows on Wapaloosie Mountain to more big views at 6 miles. The path climbs over two more mountain tops before ascending Copper Butte, 7135 feet, 13 miles.

By means of a two-car switch or a helper, a 28-mile one-way trip, the classic of the range, can be made from Sherman Pass to Boulder-Deer Creek road.

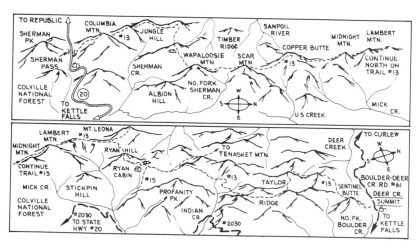

99 WHITE MOUNTAIN

Round trip 14 miles
Hiking time 8 hours
High point 6923 feet
Elevation gain 3300 feet

Hikable mid-June through
   October
One day
USGS Sherman Peak

Part of the growing-up process for local youths hereabouts used to be spending a night atop the bleached-granite summit of White Mountain, on a vision quest. Later, after visions faded in the aftermath of the European plagues and the White Wars, a fire-lookout cabin was erected and stood there from 1919 into the 1950s. Hikers of today can repeat the olden pilgrimage, renewing the quest for a vision (such as, of a Kettle Range Wilderness). For a slightly less strenuous spiritual experience they can ascend Barnaby Buttes, which had a lookout tower from 1940 to 1974.

There are two ways to White Mountain. For one (#2 on our list of recommendations) drive Highway 20 west from Kettle Falls 15 miles, to within 3.8 miles of Sherman Pass, turn off on road No. 2020 for 6.2 miles, turn left on road No. 2014 for about 4 miles to South Fork Barnaby Creek road No. 250, which in some 5 miles leads to the White Mountain trail, elevation 5100 feet.

For the other, described here, drive roads No. 2020 and No. 2014, as above. On the latter, at .3 mile from the junction, just beyond South Sherman Creek bridge, find road No. (2014)500, elevation 3600 feet.

The sign here says "Barnaby Butte Trail 2½ miles." If logging is in progress the family van may be able to drive on, as the four-by-fours always do. Most folks will do better to walk those 2½ miles (which are calculated into our mileages here) to the official trailhead, elevation 4300 feet. A sign prohibits wheels of any number from continuing on. (Ha! Ha! Ha!)

Much of the trail is along an abandoned truck road, very rough—but well-shaded, bless God's forest. At about 3½ miles (1 from the official trailhead) it crosses a goodly stream with a small campsite surrounded by signs announcing an impending clearcut. (Boo!) The way now steepens and one wonders what sort of truck ever negotiated the track.

At 5 miles, 6050 feet, the road-trail tops Kettle Ridge and intersects South Kettle Crest trail No. 13. What to do? Two choices.

For one, go right 1½ miles on the truck road-trail to the green slopes of Barnaby Buttes and to the lookout site at 6534 feet.

For the other and better, go left along the ridge crest. In a scant 1 mile the trail tips upward, steeply at times to avoid large boulder fields. At one spot it even drops 150 feet to dodge the big rocks. At roughly 6¾ miles is a four-way intersection. Trail No. 13 continues straight ahead. Turn left to the summit of White Mountain, 6923 feet, 7 miles from where you most likely parked your family van. The views extend east to Lake Roosevelt, as the reservoirized Columbia River is known behind Grand Coulee Dam, and west to miles of rolling hills in the Kettles and the Okanogan Highlands. For more, follow the ridge northwest, weaving through patches of krummnolz to a rocky outcrop.

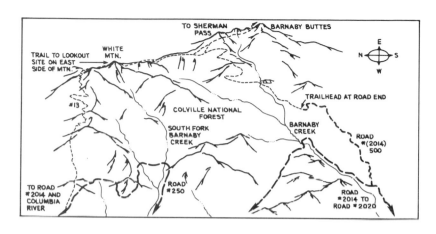

Kettle Range from White Mountain

100 PACIFIC CREST TRAIL

One-way trip Allison Pass to
Stehekin River 87 miles
Allow 10–12 days
Elevation gain 12,400 feet

Hikable August through
September

For rugged mountain scenery, the portion of the Pacific Crest National
Scenic Trail between the Canadian border and Stevens Pass is the most
spectacular long walking route in the nation. Undependable weather,
late-melting snow, and many ups and downs make it also one of the most
difficult and strenuous.

Few hikers have time to complete the trip in one season; most spread
their efforts over a period of years, doing the trail in short sections. Those
taking the whole trip at once generally prefer to start from the north,
since pickup transportation at journey's end is easier to arrange at the
south terminus. Though higher, the northern part of the trail lies in the
rainshadow of great peaks to the west and thus gets less snow than the
southern part; the north country and south country therefore open to
travel simultaneously.

There is no legal way for a hiker to cross the Canadian–U.S. border on
the Pacific Crest Trail. However, U.S. Forest Service wilderness permits
for hiking in the Pasayten Wilderness on the U.S. side of the border were
available until 1985, when they were no longer needed, at the visitors'
center in Manning Provincial Park, Canada. Hikers must draw their
own conclusion and decide whether or not to join the hundreds of folks
who cross the border on this and the Monument 83 Trail (Hike 79).

Drive the Trans-Canada Highway to Manning Provincial Park and
find the trailhead on an unmarked sideroad ½ mile east of the hotel-
motel complex at Allison Pass. Hike 7½ miles up Castle Creek to the international boundary at Monument 78. Look east and west from the
monument along the corridor cleared by boundary survey crews; in recent years the new growth has been cut or sprayed. Ascend Route Creek
to Castle Pass, from which point south to Harts Pass the trail is almost
continuously in meadowland, touching Hopkins Pass, climbing to
Lakeview Ridge, crossing Woody Pass into Conie Basin and Rock Pass
into Goat Lakes Basin, dropping to Holman Pass, swinging around Jim
Mountain to Jim Pass, Foggy Pass, and Oregon Basin, crossing a
shoulder of Tamarack Peak into Windy Basin, and from there continuing
to Harts Pass as described in Hike 76. **Distance from Allison Pass to
Harts Pass 40 miles, elevation gain about 8000 feet, hiking time 4
days.**

From Harts Pass the next road junction is at Rainy Pass. The trail con-
tours around Tatie Peak to Grasshopper Pass (Hike 74), drops to Glacier
Pass, drops more into the West Fork Methow River, climbs over Methow
Pass, and contours high around Tower Mountain to Granite Pass and on

Pacific Crest Trail

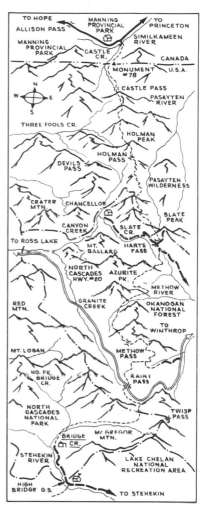

to Cutthroat Pass and down to Rainy Pass (Hikes 68 and 66). **Distance from Harts Pass to Rainy Pass 31 miles, elevation gain about 4400 feet, hiking time 4 days.**

The next segment is all downhill along Bridge Creek to the Stehekin River road. Walk east to the Rainy Lake—Bridge Creek trail and descend forest to the road at Bridge Creek Campground (Hike 48). Hike 5 miles down the Stehekin River road to High Bridge Campground. **Distance from Rainy Pass to High Bridge 16 miles, hiking time 2 days.**

To continue south, see *100 Hikes in the Glacier Peak Region.*

STILL MORE HIKES IN THE NORTH CASCADES

This book covers the 180 miles west-east from slopes of Mt. Baker to the Kettle Range and the 40 miles from Cascade Pass to Canada. Companion volumes, *100 Hikes in the (Glacier Peak) North Cascades, 100 Hikes in the Alpine Lakes, 50 Hikes in Mount Rainier National Park* and *100 Hikes in the South Cascades and Olympics,* reach south. Another, *103 Hikes in the Southwestern British Columbia,* follows the North Cascades over the border to their end. Shorter walks than those herein are described in *Trips and Trails 1: Family Camps, Short Hikes, and View Roads around the North Cascades.* The interface of Western Washington lowlands and front ridges of the Cascades is treated in *Footsore 3: Walks and Hikes Around Puget Sound.* Approaches to and routes up peaks are the subject of *Cascade Alpine Guide,* a series of three volumes.

The 100 hikes have been selected to be representative of all the varied provinces of the (far) North Cascades and neighboring ranges to the east. However, it's a big country with many other comparable trips. The books noted above describe many. Following is a sampling—some covered by the books, some not—that can be particularly recommended. The lack of detailed recipes may be compensated for by greater solitude.

NOOKSACK RIVER

Silesia Creek from Canada: Reached from logging roads—lovely, if brushy, forest walk. Also accessible from Twin Lakes.

Bastille Ridge: Spectacular view of Coleman Glacier reached after a difficult river crossing.

Chilliwack River from Canada: Excellent forest walk from Chilliwack Lake.

Price Lake: Climbers' path to rock-milky lake under Price Glacier.

BAKER RIVER

Baker Lake Shore: 3-mile trail on east side of lake. Find trail 1 mile north of dam.

Anderson Lakes, Watson Lakes, and Anderson Butte: See *Trips and Trails 1.*

Dock Butte: See *Trips and Trails 1.*

Blue Lake: ¾-mile walk. See Trips and Trails 1.

Slide Lake: Easy 1-mile hike from road No. 16. See the massive rockslide that dammed the lake.

SKAGIT RIVER—ROSS LAKE

Sauk Mountain: See *Trips and Trails 1.*

Diablo Lake trail: From Diablo Dam above cliffs to Ross Lake.

Ruby Creek: Magnificent river walk near North Cascades Highway.

Ruby Mountain: Abandoned trail, long climb, but spectacular views for the experienced hiker.

Perry Creek: Sidetrip on virtually vanished trail from Little Beaver into a hanging valley.

Silver Creek: Unmaintained valley trail on the west side of Ross Lake.
McAllister Creek: Dead-end trail from Thunder Creek.

CASCADE RIVER

Marble Creek: See *Trips and Trails 1*.
Trapper Lake: Rough trail to a deep cirque east of Cascade Pass.

LAKE CHELAN—STEHEKIN RIVER

Flat Creek: Dead-end, 3⅓-mile trail into a scenic valley under the LeConte Glacier, giving access to a tough cross-country trip to the Ptarmigan Traverse.
Rainbow Lake: Popular trail to alpine lake.
Junction Mountain: Dead-end trail with views of Agnes and Stehekin valleys.
Prince Creek, Canoe Creek, Fish Creek: Long, steep access trails from Lake Chelan to the Chelan Summit.
Boulder Creek: To War Creek Pass and Chelan Summit.

TWISP RIVER

Hoodoo Pass: Into the heart of the Chelan Summit.
Fish Creek Pass: Long, easy hike up Buttermilk Creek to Chelan Summit.
War Creek: A much easier trail to War Creek Pass than the grueling approach from Stehekin.
Reynolds Creek: Joins the Boulder Creek trail.
North Creek: Steep, dry trial to a tiny mountain lake or down Cedar Creek to Early Winters.
Oval Creek: To small alpine lakes under the Chelan Crest.

METHOW RIVER

Wolf Creek: Long valley trail to Gardner Meadows, continuing to old mines and the summits of Gardner Mountain and Abernathy Peaks.
Baron Creek: From Chancellor.
Beaver Creek: This trail near Winthrop has been drastically shortened by logging roads.
Foggy Dew Ridge: A forest walk to viewpoint.
Gardner Mountain: A high ridge walk.
Lookout Mountain: Trail to lookout. See *Trips and Trails 1*.
Pearrygin Creek: Drastically shortened by logging roads.
Setting Sun Mountain: Old lookout site on edge of Pasayten Wilderness.

EARLY WINTERS CREEK

Silver Star: Mud Lake a hunters' camp reached by blazed route from Cedar Creek trail.
Early Winters: Remnants of trail not obliterated by Highway 20.
Willow Creek: Climbers' route to camp on Silver Star Mountain.

GRANITE CREEK

East Creek-Mebee Pass: Steep climb on old Indian-miners' route.
Mill Creek-Azurite Pass: Stiff climb beginning on an old mining road.
Granite Creek: Remnants of trail not obliterated by Highway 20.
Cabinet Creek: Abandoned from Highway 20 to Gabriel Pass.

CHEWACK RIVER

Doe Mountain: Abandoned trail to lookout site.
Mt. Barney: Trail to alpine meadows.
Tiffany Lake: 7 miles of trail between roads Nos. 91 and 370.
Twentymile Creek: Seldom used trail to North Twentymile Meadows.
Meadow Lake: Steep sidetrail from Andrews Creek to lake and Coleman
    Peak.
Crystal Lake: 9 miles to small alpine lake.

OKANOGAN RIVER

Mt. Bonaparte: Antoine trail to lookout.
Mt. Bonaparte: South Side trail to lookout from road No. (3300)100.
Pipsissewa Point: Two miles to viewpoint of Bonaparte Lake. Also
    reached by road No. (3300)100.

KETTLE RANGE

Thirteen Mountain: Difficult to follow to Thirteenmile Mountain and
    Thirteenmile Basin.
South Kettle Range: A ridge walk south of Sherman Pass.

INDEX